£6·50

THE MUSIC OF A

D0659622

The Music of
ALEXANDER GOEHR

Interviews and Articles
Edited by Bayan Northcott

Edition 11486
ISBN 0 901938 05 X

Schott & Co. Ltd.
48 Gt. Marlborough Street,
London W1V 2BN

The editor and publishers are grateful to the individual authors for use of their copyright material in this book (Interviews I and II are copyright of the editor).

Contents

Preface and Acknowledgments

Although most of Alexander Goehr's major works are discussed in the following pages, the primary purpose of this symposium is less to offer a systematic analysis of his output than to suggest the range and evolution of his ideas both in, and about, music over the quarter of a century since his work first began to attract attention – ideas which, to speak for myself and, I believe, many of the other contributors, have proved more consistently serious, stimulating and independent than those of any other British musician of his generation. These 'notes towards a musical portrait' are therefore of varied provenance. The two interviews with Goehr himself, together with Bill Hopkins' article on the piano music, Melanie Daiken on the *Triptych,* Peter-Paul Nash on the chamber music, Julian Rushton on the orchestral music and Robin Holloway's avowedly personal critique, have all been specially commissioned. Hugh Wood's survey of the choral music, however, appeared as long as fourteen years ago in *The American Choral Review* (viii/2 1965, p 6), David Drew's *Why Must Arden Die?* is a revised and greatly-expanded version of two articles which appeared in *The Listener* (lxxviii, 1967, pp 412, 445) and my own piece, *The Recent Music,* is a slightly revised conflation of two articles first published in *Tempo* in 1978 (No. 124, p 10 and 125, p 12). I am most grateful to the Editors of these publications for permission to reprint, likewise to Universal Edition for the Bartók music example on p 52. Finally, my very best thanks to the staff at Schott: to John Collins for overseeing the production, to Clifford Caesar for note-setting the music examples, to David Stevens for help in proof-reading and to Sally Groves without whose encouragement and powers of persuasion this book might never have appeared.

Bayan Northcott
June 1979

Biographical Note

Alexander Goehr was born in Berlin on 10 August 1932, son of the conductor, Walter Goehr, who brought his family to England early in 1933. He was educated at Berkhamsted School and studied composition with Richard Hall at the Royal Manchester College of Music (1952-5), founding the New Music Manchester Group during this time with his fellow students Peter Maxwell Davies, Harrison Birtwistle, Elgar Howarth and John Ogdon. He spent the academic year 1955-6 in Paris on a French Government scholarship, attending Messiaen's master class at the Conservatoire and studying strict counterpoint privately with Yvonne Loriod. On his return to London he earned his living mainly as a copyist and translator until 1960, when he joined the BBC as a producer of orchestral concerts, a post he held until 1968, during which period he also organised the Wardour Castle Summer School of Music in 1964 and 1965 with Davies and Birtwistle. After spending the summer of 1968 in Tokyo on a Churchill Scholarship, he was Composer-in-Residence at the New England Conservatory, Boston, for the academic year 1968-9, and for the following year he was Associate Professor of music at Yale University. In 1970-71, he was a visiting lecturer at Southampton University, which conferred upon him its first honorary doctorate in music in 1973. From 1967-72, he was also musical director of the Music Theatre Ensemble. He was appointed West Riding Professor and Head of the Music Department at Leeds University in 1971, also directing the Leeds Musical Festival of 1976. He was appointed Professor of Music at the University of Cambridge in 1976. In addition to his published catalogue of some 40 works, Goehr has written a quantity of incidental music, conducted, broadcast and taught many younger composers, including Anthony Gilbert, Roger Smalley and Robin Holloway. He has twice married and has three daughters and a son.

Interview 1:
Towards the Little Symphony

Bayan Northcott: You are sometimes described as a Schoenbergian, though Messiaen and Boulez have also affected your development. Yet I have often heard you say that your father remains a major influence upon you.

Alexander Goehr: Both my parents were – or are – musicians. My father was a conductor who had started life wanting to be a composer and had been in Schoenberg's masterclass in Berlin. Later he also conducted operetta. Advanced music – Schoenberg, Bartók and Stravinsky – as well as light music mixed together in my childhood to form a rather extraordinary idea of what music was. Schoenberg and Duke Ellington rubbed shoulders in our home but I did not know too much about Mozart and Haydn; they were not in my father's repertoire in those years. My mother trained as a pianist at the Kiev Conservatory. Horowitz was her neighbour. Later she was in the masterclass at the Berlin Hochschule, a pupil of Scharwenka and Leonid Kreutzer and a contemporary of Claudio Arrau. She played mainly Chopin, Tchaikovsky and, sometimes, duets with my father (including the occasional Mahler symphony). We had gramophone records in the house but they were mostly factory pressings of my father's recordings and although there were some classics among them – a famous recording of the Tchaikovsky piano concerto with Egon Petri, for instance – a lot of them were opera arias with well-known singers whom my father accompanied. My basic musical fare was this rather casual selection of music, together with the sounds of the hammering-out of a great deal of wartime propaganda music through the ceiling of my father's study (above which I tried to sleep). I was 'just' born in Berlin (in 1932) but I was brought to England when I was three or four months old, so that England and English were my first home and language, though I speak German too.

BN: When and how did you start composing?

AG: Little notebooks of Red Indian marches have survived written at about 6 or 7. I had music lessons very early on and, at various points, studied violin, clarinet and piano, but all this went astray and by the age of 10 or 11, I had stopped learning completely. I really started composing – though with very little idea of how to go about it – when I was 13 or 14. My first piece was a setting of the *Preludes* of T. S. Eliot for voice and string quartet – I also wrote poetry at that time which I suspect to have been very bad, but happily it has not survived. I first saw myself as a composer around the age of 15,

when I wrote a piano suite, very obviously modelled on Stravinsky's Sere-
nade in A. But I kept these efforts very much out of my father's way and out
of the way of conventional music teaching at my school. I did not feel
then that I connected with other people who were 'musical' and what I did, I
did secretively. My choice of texts often related to my studies in Greek and
Latin — a lot of my pieces were settings of Catullus and Horace. The crisis
came for me around the age of 18 when I announced that I wanted to study
music. Of course, by that time I was very far behind — I just did not have the
necessary equipment. I took some lessons with Henry Geehl, a very eminent
man in his day — he had been Elgar's amanuensis at the time of *The Dream of
Gerontius*. He taught me piano, harmony and counterpoint for a while and I
learnt a very great deal from him but could not stay with him for long.

BN: Having won a place at Oxford to study classics, you first had to do your
National Service, which meant working in mental hospitals and on the land
(since you were a conscientious objector), and which, in turn, was to take
you to Manchester instead, where you found not only a remarkable generation of contemporaries but a remarkable teacher as well.

AG: Yes, Manchester — a dark town — but I had a few introductions from my
father and it was through the pianist, Iso Elinson, that I found my way to
Richard Hall, who not only agreed to teach me, but who took me seriously —
as my father had not up to that time. Michael Tippett had looked at early
pieces and given me a lot of encouragement. He was the first person who told
me the rather English thing that the best reason for doing something was
because you wanted to do it; whereas my father's more German approach was
that the best reason for doing something was that you were good at it. I was
manifestly *not* good at it, so I was very pleased to be told that I should try all
the same. Max Deutsche, a Schoenberg pupil still living in Paris, also gave very
valuable advice. These were people my father got in to discourage me and
who, to some extent, did the opposite. But Richard Hall was the man who
helped me tremendously, not only through lessons, but personally. He was
not a teacher with whom one sat down and did harmony exercises in the
conventional sense. I think he was too bored by the hundreds of unwilling
instrumentalists he had had to teach and glad when someone came along
wanting to talk about real things — so perhaps we were a bit short on formal
teaching. But there was no degree course for composers, so it hardly mattered
('they' wanted one to take the piano teacher's diploma, but I never turned
up).

But then the Old Manchester College was very different at that time from
the Royal College and Academy. Many of the teachers had been pupils of
Petri, including Dora Gilson, who taught me piano — she was a fine lady who
knew a great deal about music and had tremendous verve. And just before I
came there had been a big Busoni thing going, through Ronald Stevenson and
others. I think I was probably responsible for moving the class on, so to

speak, to Schoenberg and Messiaen. In fact, Manchester was a good place for a young composer to be because – like a German provincial town – it encouraged a kind of romantic aspiration which was not just laughed at. Something of the old Hallé tradition was still going in the place, shabby as it was. I was very happy, not only with my teachers and fellow students, but precisely because new music was still new and shocking there. We *had* to put on concerts of our own music, and it was all rather good because it meant something. It was the beginning of the 1950s and there was a rising spirit of optimism; and since many of the students were demobilised ex-servicemen, there was an air of seriousness too. Of course I was lucky in my contemporaries, not only Peter Maxwell Davies, Harrison Birtwistle, John Ogdon and Elgar Howarth, but a number of others who have not become known as composers and performers but who were very thoughtful and interesting. There was one composer, whom I liked particularly, who used to compose what we called 'Manchester Spanish' – like Albéniz – and another who tied himself in knots with the Schillinger system of mathematical processes; it was all very stimulating and enjoyable. The cross-fertilisation of these things with Richard Hall as catalyst, and then the excitement of the first visit to London of Messiaen and Yvonne Loriod in connection with the British première of *Turangalîla* (under my father) – and an occasion after the performance at Felix Aprahamian's house, when Loriod played the Boulez Second Sonata and Messiaen played rhythmic clapping games with us – these, and my father's Schoenbergian enthusiasms all mixed together to produce my particular range of interests.

BN: To what extent did you and your contemporaries share interests in the rhythmic and proportional techniques of, for instance, Indian or Medieval music at this time?

AG: Richard Hall was very interested in Indian music and so was Maxwell Davies who wrote his University dissertation about it. None of us had heard much; it was before the days of the arrival of Ali Akbah Khan and our interest was theoretical. But then, I found endless fascination in the Henry Watson Library in Manchester; its librarian, the splendid and always encouraging John Russell had bought really well throughout the inter-war years, the place was stuffed with stimulating music and my reading took in Oriental and Medieval texts as well as everything else. What was new then was that our situation as composers made it possible, perhaps, to find ways of harnessing these esoteric interests. Fairly early on I studied certain Medieval techniques (or what I thought to be Medieval techniques, because one could never be sure whether one was getting them quite right) and some of my pieces at that time were concerned with ornamenting lines. This became very important in Maxwell Davies' earliest pieces, and indeed, to some extent, in Birtwistle's too. I was trying to extend classical 12-tone technique into a quasi-modal dimension.

BN: Nonetheless, this casting around for techniques represented something of a new spirit in British music.

AG: Yes and no. On the one hand, there was all the excitement of the early years of Darmstadt, of Boulez, Nono and Stockhausen seeping through from foreign radio stations; even if, as it now seems, these composers were not so much innovators as re-discoverers of earlier innovations. On the other hand, Manchester was still basically very conservative and we were trying to write pieces there. It was just before the time when one was proud to be called avant-garde; to be called that meant brickbats rather than bouquets. While a man such as Richard Hall was interested in the methodology of serialism, rhythmic cells and so on, he felt — possibly under the influence of war-time music and the English situation — that it was desirable to bend these new techniques to fundamentally traditional purposes. The ideas of bending and decorating 12-tone technique were really ways of creating a milder kind of music than that practised abroad. But there was a clean break between us and the immediately preceding generation of Fricker, Hamilton and Milner. They were still working within an expanded tonal situation with Hindemith and Bartók as the immediate influences, whereas the Manchester students under the influence of Richard Hall — even though I do not think he liked Schoenberg very much — were the first in England to take the ethos of Schoenberg and Webern (and Messiaen, when he arrived) dead seriously — apart from Elisabeth Lutyens. Incidentally, I owe some of my earliest encouragement to that fine and generous lady.

BN: It was the 'arrival' of Messiaen that decided you to study in Paris?

AG: Yes, but it was some years before I had the opportunity. I was still only a second-year student at the time of the *Turangalila* performance. Of course we were all shattered — I defy anyone at 20 not to be shattered — by what seemed a totally fresh ethos, and perhaps we realised instinctively that what was going on in Paris then was quite new. But I had more or less absorbed the Messiaen influence by the time I actually got to Paris. Yvonne Loriod thought my early Piano Sonata showed an intuitive understanding of the structure of Messiaen's language. I think she smiled on that piece more than any music of mine she has seen since. By the time I was in Messiaen's class at the Conservatoire, I had already begun to react against his musical language; partly because it did not fit in with what was developing into the concept of total serialism, partly because of its embarrassing religiosity, and partly because, although I recognised him as a great man, I was reverting to my real interest in Schoenberg. I could never throw that off — the more I looked at other things, the more enthusiastic I became about him. That has always remained — though I am the only Schoenbergian I know who has been submitted to French harmony teaching and this also had a very strong effect upon me.

Boulez was still living in Paris while I was a student there. John Carewe and I used to visit him quite often — once a fortnight or so — and although we never took lessons as such, he was very generous with his time. We spent afternoons with him looking at Webern, Debussy or Berg scores and generally talking about music. I certainly regarded him as by far the most striking of the Darmstadt composers – very much the leader at that time, and I held him in awe because the effect of his Second Sonata on me was overpowering. I think it still is – it is a superb achievement. And those were also the years of *Le Marteau sans Maître* and the Domaine Musicale. He had as big an influence upon me as Messiaen, but it was not, I feel, entirely a positive influence. I had written a number of things, including an orchestral piece, before I went to Paris. But I could not really compose while I was there and in the two or three years after I returned to London, I was rather inhibited by taking, perhaps too literally, the strange mixture that characterises his thinking of an aspiration towards the expressively new with a rigorous discipline, almost – dare I say it? – an academicism, which appeals only too greatly to me who has that tendency too.

People tend to group composers, superficially, according to whether they are more or less 'modern-sounding'. I am surely considered nowadays among the less 'modern-sounding'. But I think there is another division. There are composers who are concerned with rigorous, problem-solving, formal composition, who like the carrying out of complex schemes and are interested in structural device for its own sake (in a sense, the academically-minded ones). Boulez is certainly such a one, as were Schoenberg, Webern and Dallapiccola; and Robert Simpson, if you like, is also such a composer, but in a quite different way! On the other hand, there are the composers who are more directly expressive – Scriabin, for instance, or even Lutoslawski and Berio and many of today's avant-garde. It is a question of musical type. In this sense, I feel more linked to Boulez by the common interest in structural device. I do not really think that divisions based upon style are that important. I like fugues and chaconnes, whether they are thought advanced or not. This is not to say that expression is unimportant to me. But I believe expression is involuntary and arises as a by-product of intellectual effort: you should think consciously of technical things – the expressive content will look after itself! In that sense, I am very much in sympathy with the Schoenbergian attitude and with the early aesthetic of someone like Boulez. I do now find that of Messiaen more questionable.

But, to return to my years after Paris – it was only really with *The Deluge* that I began to find my way back into composition.

BN: The first performance was conducted by your father. Did this signify his blessing at last upon your work?

AG: Well, relations with my father had always blown hot and cold. He did get very interested in what I was doing. This took the form either of extremely negative harangues about how bad he thought my pieces were, or grudging approval (which was the most one could ever get out of him). He did *The*

Deluge and actually secured for me my first successful performance, and one that made something of an impression. He helped me with all my pieces right up to his death, giving very specific proposals about re-harmonising this or re-setting that. He was particularly good on notation; on the best ways to write things down. But he had to tamper with everything; he was a Gemini and loved alternatives. *The Deluge* was the first piece in which I found something which led me forward, and that had to do with harmony. The Piano Sonata already had a conscious harmonic dimension (John Ogdon once analysed it to show it was really just a copy of the Liszt Sonata!). But whenever I have succeeded, or so it seems to me, it has always had to do with some discovery about the harmonic aspect of music so neglected in our time: the Piano Sonata, *The Deluge,* the Two Choruses, the *Little Symphony,* and most recently, my 'tonal' pieces since *Psalm IV.*

BN: Now *The Deluge* got noticed. You were even hailed in certain quarters as the leader of the first true British avant-garde – a thrusting into a public position which had consequences for you, I think.

AG: Before that, friends among the Darmstadt avant-garde – and I had many of them, Nono in particular – had rather made me feel that I should not stay in England; that the situation was not right for the music I wanted to write. When my studies in Paris had ended, I did make a rather feeble attempt, under the influence of the inter-war Paris expatriates – Joyce, Hemingway, Durrell – to stay. René Leibowitz very kindly gave me some paid work, but I had no real means of supporting myself, my wife at that time hated France and things became very difficult. So I finally came back although I was still not sure about staying here. But then the musical scene began to take a more optimistic turn, at the ICA and the SPNM and with William Glock's accession at the BBC. I succeeded Iain Hamilton at Morley College – up to then most of my living had been from copying. Children were born. And *The Deluge* brought a whole string of commissions of which I took on three for 1961 – unwisely, because it was really too much for me and too soon. The only thing that succeeded in its own way was the Melos Ensemble piece, the Suite for sextet commissioned for the Aldeburgh Festival. It was composed very much at the personal prompting of Britten who wrote to me in his own fair hand asking for a divertimento-type piece including flute and harp. When I objected that this seemed far away from my current stylistic preoccupations, he replied that this was precisely why he thought I ought to take it on. He was quite right; it did open up new possibilities for me.

But the Proms piece, *Hecuba's Lament,* was put together from bits of an opera I had been working on – which is not the way to fulfil one's first major orchestral commission – and of course the really traumatic commission was the Leeds Festival piece, *Sutter's Gold.* I encouraged myself not to be too concerned with its practicality, partly from an anti-conventional attitude of 'Let them have it' and partly from my simple lack of knowledge about how to write for a big chorus. I still hold to the piece; I think it has some interesting music in it and I would like to hear it again, because now it would not be so difficult to perform. But at the time, the chorus master was obviously so completely bemused by something which was quite outside his experience, that, instead of just saying, 'We can't sing this', he carried on and the performance was an almost unmitigated disaster. I was helped through by John Pritchard, who just saved my skin, and I am not a person who gets immediately knocked down by that sort of thing, but afterwards I felt very badly about the dislike of those singers I had made do something they loathed doing – it was not practical, it was not well-written for chorus – and I resolved never to do anything like it again until I was sure how to do it. So that though I was the first of my generation to get such public exposure, I did not use it well. I needed the advice of an older composer perhaps – because, you know, styles come and styles go but a young composer needs someone to show him the ropes who knows about the pacing and timing of composing, quite apart from the content.

BN: Though Hanns Eisler, whom you presumably met through your father, was to help you in this way over the next year?

AG: Yes, he was a great professional and technician who had done everything – and a very wise man. I saw a lot of him around then and became very fond of him, and I learned a great deal from him too. I think David Blake's continuing enthusiasm for him as a teacher testifies to the same thing. I remember him saying after we had been listening to a tape of my Suite: "Very nice, very sensitive and all that, but real composers write pieces which are in big arcs and you must attempt something like a sonata form." He also pulled me away from the narrower, more modish avant-garde world. I had never entirely been at ease with what was going on at Darmstadt. But I was sympathetic to the spirit of it. I liked to go there and argue over what Boulez, Stockhausen or Nono were doing at the time because I agreed with the way they delineated the problems; I did not always agree with their solutions. But by this time, the influence of Cage at Darmstadt was changing something that, from my point of view, was serious, into something less serious, and I parted company with it more and more.

BN: You dedicated your next work, the Two Choruses, to the memory of Eisler, but it also surely represented a major step forward of your own?

AG: I was naturally very sensitive about choral writing and anxious to get it right – though getting it right for the professionals of the John Alldis Choir was a very different story from my friends in Leeds. John Alldis' appearance on our new music scene – he was brought in by Malcolm Williamson – was something of a phenomenon. Here was this typical King's College and light music sort of fellow who suddenly got himself crossed with the English avant-garde. He brought out a kind of showbiz element, which, of course, he deliberately cultivated, in the composers with whom he worked. I had recently joined the BBC and spent a lot of time looking through the choral pieces of Schoenberg, Stravinsky, Janáček and Eisler for things for him to put into his programmes — which he did; they were the best possible programmes for a small choir. And I learnt something from working with him; he convinced me of the importance of making a special choral 'sound'. This led me to a further adaptation of my 12-tone technique which simply *worked*; a kind of doubling and redundancy technique which produced the effect you first hear as a choral 'splash' near the beginning of the Two Choruses. In fact, this harked back to something which interested Richard Hall: a combination of serial and modal technique derived, I think, from Krenek. Only now I suddenly found in it a rich seam which I quarried for the first time on a large scale in my next piece, the *Little Symphony*, written in memory of my father, and which was to be a major preoccupation of my music for the next 15 years.

BN: And it was the *Little Symphony* which first embodied the unmistakable harmonic ambience of the mature Goehr.

AG: Well, maybe.

The Piano Music

BILL HOPKINS

In distinct contrast to the works with orchestra, the solo piano music seeks out forms appropriate to a distillation of the composer's thought, at the same time as liberating certain aspects of that thought from the constraints of ensemble playing. To this extent the piano fulfils a traditional role as the composer's most intimate and most accommodating confidant, and its importance in Goehr's output is accordingly of a very special kind. Any one of his four works for solo piano would make a rewarding and useful piece for a pianist proposing a serious venture into contemporary styles and techniques. All are fairly demanding on manual and mental dexterity, but none sets fearsome interpretative riddles, since the music is always direct in its expression. Individually the works are as varied in form as they are in intention, something of which can be gleaned from their titles. The Sonata, Op. 2 (1952), whose date alone declares it a student work, explores ways of developing contrasted material in a single movement; the Capriccio, Op. 6 (1957), works with reduced material in the interests of a more Webernian dialectic; the Three Pieces, Op. 18 (1964), one of Goehr's most personal works, exhibits interrelated musical objects of considerable poetic pregnancy; and *Nonomiỹa*, Op. 27 (1969), mobilizes its objects to articulate a ritual sequence. For each work the composer has coined its own highly distinctive material, though all are very obviously aspects of a single creative personality and its development.

Much of the Sonata seems to have been conceived as a work for right hand with left-hand accompaniment, such is the bias with which thematic material is distributed. This feature is symptomatic of the writing's indebtedness to the pianism of Prokofiev, who is commemorated by an inscription in the published edition of the work, and whose Seventh Sonata is directly invoked towards the end of it. Octaves, fifteenths, twenty-seconds and double octaves appear, sometimes as timbres, sometimes as textural reinforcement. Nostalgic use is made of irregular rhythms built over short, regular ostinato figures. Consideration has clearly been given to what will fit pleasantly under the hands, and the muscles are taxed and stretched typically at tense, climactic passages in the music. Climaxing itself is generally effected with the aid of centrifugal pitch sequences, often of marked internal regularity: the work's last climax, for instance, is prepared by three fan-like anacruses with the right hand rising in parallel seconds, in parallel thirds, and ultimately in parallel tritones.

What Prokofiev would not have envisaged is the work's musical language, which is firmly anchored to the principle of chromatic complementarity. The four opening chords suggest a Schoenbergian series of rich intervallic potential, offering convincing variety within audible unity, its two hexachords neatly built of major seconds and minor thirds (if allowance is made for a simple permutation by which two tritones in a diminished-seventh formation can be converted into minor thirds too): 2M - 4 - T - 3m - T; and 3m - 2M - 3m - 3m - 2M. The only alien interval is the perfect fourth, a fact the composer acknowledges by segregating the row's first two notes to make a drumming motive — Ex. 1. Within four statements, with no more than octave transpositions, the row is already made to yield the music's basic harmonic, textural, rhythmic and motivic subject matter in a kind of miniature development and recapitulation. There is even a characteristically fastidious dynamic profiling of the 'exposition' statement, though the work will not be so expressionistic as this rapid sequence of sharp contrasts seems to promise. The scale on which the composition is conceived is too broad for this, as well as for the free and independent application of the normal serial principle of constant transposition.

Ex. 1

Maestoso

Instead, the series is used thematically, as a quarry which will provide a variety of recognizable pitch configurations for use over the broad expanses traditionally associated with sonata form. Detached fragments appear as ostinati, a retrograde and even a deformed original *(lento, quasi parlando)* emerge as melodic entities, and the row's characteristic intervallic groupings can be heard in the harmonies. The underlying complementarity gives the harmonies an atonal feel, but their frequent composition of seconds and thirds savours of the modally derived complexes of Messiaen. A more overt link with the French composer appears in Goehr's skilful adaptations of additive rhythmic structures, both towards a certain lyrical freedom in the thematic writing and as a means of leavening the motoric impulse of his developments with witty variants. When the opening notes of Prokofiev's Seventh Sonata erupt in the recapitulation section, they lack both the tempo and the character of the original: this is a symbolic allusion rather than a literal quotation. The act of homage is further accentuated by its contextual gratuity – it has neither formal nor serial inherence; only in isolated respects (two trichords of the row, monodic writing in octaves) does it appear specifically germane. It would be surprising at that date if a further towering influence, that of Bartók, did not haunt the Sonata, notably where pitch identity spills over into percussive noise. But to have subsumed such influences is part of Goehr's real achievement in the work, and only adds to the impressiveness of its coherence and originality.

Capriccio appeared after Goehr's period of study with Messiaen and of direct contact with Parisian avant-garde of the time. It is dedicated to Yvonne Loriod – an exponent of Webern and Boulez as well as of Messiaen. The sharper focus of the work's pitch content is immediately in evidence: minor seconds and major thirds are now the principal elements, combining in addition or subtraction to form the secondary intervals of a fourth and a minor third. Thematic pitch content has vanished, and three- and four-note cells have become the norm. They are pitted against each other in constant transpositions so that, despite its relatively complex interplay of serial forms, this music probably represents Goehr's nearest approach to the strict avoidance of pitch repetition as practised by the Viennese serialists. There is, however, a tendency – not typical of other post-Webernian music of the period – for rhythmic articulation to preserve the intervallic identity of these pitch cells. Apart from periodic surges in which the rhythmic tissue becomes more connective, the work's rhythms too result from a polyphony of cellular fragments, each subject to the types of variation systematized by Messiaen, but again (notably in the *scherzando* passages) tending to fall into recognizable patterns.

These recurring identities, as well as the indicated repeat embracing virtually the entire piece, point to a specifically Webernian perception of musical form. There are other, more remarkable acquisitions in Capriccio. Goehr's masterly handling of tempo fluidity adds a new dimension to his music's wit (a preponderant factor in this work). Dynamic detail is filled in with assurance, exaggerating the piece's explosive volatility. Finally, the writing for the instrument has become extraordinarily free. Both hands range widely over the keyboard; they execute sizable leaps, frequently interlock or cross, and are called on to achieve the greatest subtlety in touch and tone, including the sustaining of harmonics, and thus are now necessarily equal participants in the musical argument. Taken in conjunction with dynamics and tempo, the writing is quite aggressively athletic; this is the most difficult of the four works. But the advance it represents is a real and lasting one.

The penchant Goehr showed in his earlier pieces for splitting up his rows into distinct motivic units gradually crystallized into a highly evolved personal method of pitch generation. The usual serial procedures of inversion and retrogradation are retained, but in addition to the permitted trans-positions of the original series, Goehr derives further pitch material from a harmonic reduction of it.[1] This approach extends the organizational pro-perties of serial technique to cover a wider stock of material, and at the same time has the decisive advantage of admitting identical serial fragments into a broader variety of contextual situations – whether they are to be used as recognizable motives or not. The use of such fragments as constants, iden-tities not to be dissolved away by the generative process, is what ultimately arrests that process. The technique thus respects the serial idea of the unity of musical space whilst reserving the right to structure that space unequally, perhaps even hierarchically. Aesthetically, the presence of a serial principle can no longer be detected in Goehr's works after the Three Pieces (one of the earliest instances of the new technique); and their abandonment of both complementarity and non-repetition similarly isolates them from the 'lin-guistic' traditions of serialism. The technique is felt above all as a stylistic control.

Texturally, the Three Pieces once more make operational distinctions between melody and harmony, and their dynamic markings emphatically suggest foreground and background zones. But between these areas Goehr has established a degree of fluidity which has caused the work to be described as 'impressionistic'; the composer himself has mentioned Debussy as an aesthetic model. In the first piece a contrast between monodic and homophonic writing 'resolves' into a polyphonic conclusion. The form is sectional, recalling the composer's interest in construction by means of juxtaposed blocks; and here the blocks represent different types of writing and their degrees of inter-penetration. The initial monodic and homophonic blocks are notably static in conception, the former characterized by narrow pitch movement and equal durations of events, the latter by 'bitonal' harmonies and regular alternation of two unequal rhythmic values. The harmonies consist of symmetrically built hexachords, each reducible to two superimposed triads (one major and one minor) arranged in varying positions; this harmonic homogeneity is naturally the outcome of Goehr's special technique of clotted serial proliferation. The regularity of the music's movement emphasizes the purely statistical charac-teristics of each block – a feature the composer is able to incorporate into the formal processes themselves. For instance, whereas the first block con-tains a repeated four-fold event, the second repeats a sequence of six har-monies (the first two being identical). The interaction between these binary and ternary 'macrorhythms' is not the least striking feature of the piece's subsequent evolution – Ex. 2.

The prominent falling semitone of the second piece governs the oscil-lations of its statically built sonorities, enlivened more by a central section

1. For further explanation, see *The Recent Music* p. 90 (Ed).

Ex. 2

of high-register chimes (each having a different duration) than by variation in the arpeggiated treatment of the harmonies, though this too is used to telling structural effect. The final piece adapts a seven-note serial fragment as the ground of a passacaglia, several of whose fifteen sections are grouped in complementary pairs. This format provides an ideal pretext for a virtuosic exhibition of the new technique's potential for unifying an evolutive musical form, both horizontally and vertically. It is a toccata-like movement incorporating an impressive range of character and texture. Starting with an exploration of simple methods of combining melody with harmony, it moves through increasingly dense writing built over pedals (6-8) to a section of linear polyphony (9) almost in the manner of the Capriccio, which makes witty capital out of mirror images. The eleventh section, redolent in its turn of the Sonata, begins a sequence of ostinato patterns which become merged with the melodic development as they thicken vertically; finally only chordal writing remains. In recognition of the renewed prominence here of harmonic and motivic discourse, Goehr takes pains to establish homogeneous backgrounds in his treatment of rhythm, metre, texture, register and dynamics; the work's greater stability in these respects allows the performer to devote more of his attention to the music's breadth and variety of expressive content.

Nonomiÿa was written at the same period as the theatrical *Triptych* and, though in no sense programmatic, was in part suggested by a Nō play in which the protagonist of the first act reappears in the second as his own ghost. Its form correspondingly consists of a preliminary 'kind of aria' followed by a second movement in which music of a 'threatening' character culminates in a 'dance'. (These descriptions, referring to the Nō play, are taken from the composer's introductory note). The intervallic constants which form the core of the piece's serial apparatus are presented with aggressive insistence, and — as is appropriate in such a dramatically gestural work — much of the emphasis is switched to rhythmic invention, here noticeably very much freer than in the Three Pieces. In addition, the writing is deliberately more florid and showy; it has a stylized, objective brilliance which throws into relief the ritualistic contrasts the work encompasses — between, for instance, embellished cantilena style and the stark rhythmic composition of the closing pages. The textures (and their distribution between the hands) are more successfully homogenized than in any of the previous piano works (Ex. 3). Consequently the instrument ceases to be a mechanical vehicle for musical thought, and becomes a persona, a protagonist in the drama, even though Goehr rightly insists that the piece does not depict, it enacts.

Ex. 3

The work's spacious paragraphs are sustained by melodic writing of unusual continuity, which is commented on and occasionally interrupted by mimic gestures from the 'accompaniment'. The rhythmic framework is strongly characterized, and particularly interesting use is made of cells in the first movement, where the seeds are sown for the work's final dramatic tension between equal and unequal notes. There is again a certain opposition of forms. The first movement is a ternary structure articulated by means of rhythmic and harmonic parallelisms; to some extent it ends by establishing a synthesis of its thematic substance. The second movement is evolutionary, passing through a series of clearly defined phases, each with its own metrical and textural characteristics. In certain respects this sequence of stable form followed by evolutionary form anticipates the two-movement shape of the Piano Concerto, Op. 33 (1972), and, indeed, the scale of *Nonomiȳa* and its gestural language make it something of a bridge between the solo works and Goehr's more 'public' music − its decorative elements having their correspondences both in the Concerto and that work's more aphoristic, variation-form predecessor, the *Konzertstück*, Op. 26 (1969).

The Choral Music

HUGH WOOD

The choralists form one of the many enclaves of which English musical life is composed. The essentially amateur nature of the large choral society in its nineteenth century days of glory remains. Meanwhile the musical world has changed, and a generation of composers has grown up in England since the war whose education has made them much more familiar with the most vital developments in continental music than with the traditional motions of English music-making. In particular, they have taken for granted that the whole conception of what it is possible to write for voices has been transformed.

The two worlds came into something like head-on collision when the first choral work of Alexander Goehr, his cantata, *Sutter's Gold,* Op. 10, was given its première in Leeds in October 1961. *Sutter* is a large scale choral-orchestral work about the California gold rush of 1848, the consequent devastation of a peaceful and prosperous landscape by hordes of gold diggers, and the reaction of the legendary Sutter, a man made rich by the natural fertility of the Sacramento Valley, who now however refuses to take part in the general gold fever. It is cast in five movements. The first is, in essence, a long melisma on the word 'gold'; the second, in faster tempo with a long orchestral introduction, describes the crowds rushing 'to join the human flood' on the way to the gold fields. The third movement is in two parts: the first picturing the desolation made by the gold diggers, then 'the sound of sand in the wooden workpans'; the second, a bass solo, a description of Sutter's land falling to waste and rotting from its own fertility. The fourth movement is a vigorous fugue and the final is a slow movement marked *Notturno:* at the end Sutter 'takes refuge in the darkness of the forest.'

In style and subject-matter alike this work was miles removed from the secondhand pieties of the routine English oratorio, sufficiently so to disconcert the choir who gave it its first performance to the extent that even minimum standards of rhythmic accuracy and ensemble were not achieved: as a performance this was non-existent. At the same time, the technical difficulties of pitching intervals, the idiosyncrasies of the word setting, the use of irrational divisions of the beat (to name three most frequently encountered types of difficulty) were all mild indeed if one compares this piece with the work of some of Goehr's continental contemporaries — *Il Canto Sospeso* or *Coro di Didone* of Nono for example — and its expressive character is certainly much more straightforward and unambiguously appealing. Its potential beauties, however, must remain muted until another performance is given by a chorus of professional standard – the large-scale equivalent of the John Alldis Choir.

Goehr's first piece to be performed by the Alldis Choir was *A Little Cantata of Proverbs*, its text a number of aphorisms from Blake's *The Marriage of Heaven and Hell*. In its dimensions it stands at the opposite pole from *Sutter*. These are truly tiny pieces: the first section consists of three aphorisms, which are given 9, 10 and 5 bars respectively: the second section has four aphorisms, 9, 12, 11, and 8 bars long. The incisive and varied impressions made within these small dimensions is amazing. But the pieces are different from *Sutter* in another way, and have for this reason a particular interest in any general study of Goehr's work. Up to now his music had been totally chromatic in harmonic language, and organized by various forms of serial technique founded on classical Schoenbergian serialism; while his rhythmic vocabulary, based on techniques derived from Messiaen, had often reached heights of considerable subtlety. The *Little Cantata* starts firmly in 4/4 time and in an orthodoxly managed D Minor, and it continues throughout to be both diatonic and rhythmically direct, though still thoroughly idiosyncratic in both these respects. The dislocation of traditional harmonic procedures is no greater than in, say, neo-classical Stravinsky, though a more relevant reference would be the harmonic language of Michael Tippett.

This might of course have been a *pièce d'occasion* (it was written for the music supplement of *The Musical Times*) with no further significance beyond the immediate purpose it was intended to serve. But the readmission of triads and diatonic patterns, of symmetrical and easily grasped rhythmic formulation was to have a great importance in the enriching of this composer's language which was to be evident in the next few works to come; his Violin Concerto, Op. 13, the *Little Symphony, *Op. 15, and the *Little Music for Strings,* Op. 16. A much simplified style was obviously appropriate also for a school piece entitled *Virtutes* and described as a 'Cycle of Songs and Melodramas for chorus, piano duet and percussion, with organ, two clarinets and cello ad lib.', which Goehr wrote to commission early in 1963. Here, in common with a number of younger English composers, Goehr tackled the job of writing music for school children – music intended to be simple, but fresh and free from the clichés of conventional educational music. But even within its extreme simplicity there remain turns of phrase, rhythm and harmony which are characteristic of its composer, and the sixth chorus, 'The Burning Babe', is particularly haunting and effective.

But before the writing of *Virtutes,* the Blake cantata and its performance by the John Alldis Choir led Goehr to write choral music on a larger scale. In the autumn of 1962 he wrote his Two Choruses, Op. 14, to texts by Milton and Shakespeare. The first was a section from Book XI of *Paradise Lost* which ponders on peace and war, asking the tragic question: how comes it for 'Peace to corrupt no less than War to waste'? The conquerors after their triumph turn to live in 'pleasure, ease and sloth, Surfeit and lust'; but the vanquished, too, lose not only their freedom but also their virtue: 'cooled in zeal' they merely 'practise how to live secure, Worldly or dissolute.' Milton ends with the reflection 'The Earth shall bear More than enough, that Temperance may be tried.' The second text is the well-known 'degree' speech from *Troilus and Cressida,* Act 1, Scene 3. In a series of vivid images, Ulysses speaks of the importance of order in social and political relations: 'Take but degree away' and justice is replaced by brute power, and in the ensuing nightmare chaos 'appetite an universal wolf' lies in wait, to consume all.

The Milton text is cast as a Recitative and Allegro. The music begins with a solemn and eloquent baritone solo (Ex. 1).

Ex. 1

The words 'peace would have crowned/With length of happy days the race of Man' are taken out of his mouth by the chorus in a rapid quasi-canonic passage, whispering *leggiero* then rising to a climax; the baritone reasserts himself as if quelling the optimistic chattering, 'But I was far deceiv'd . . .' His final question 'how comes it thus?' is taken up, in minims, by the other voices one by one (Ex. 2).

Ex. 2

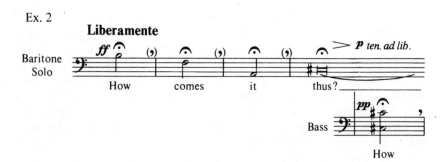

Ex. 2 cont.

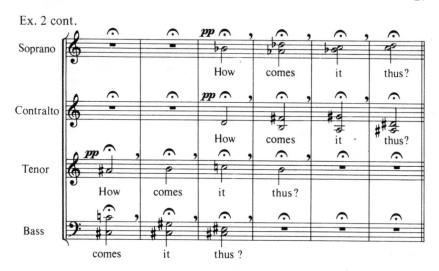

Then the Allegro begins — at first with the choir in octaves, later through a series of rapidly succeeding imitative entrances alternating with chordal passages up to a climax: 'Fame in the world, high titles and rich prey.' Ex. 3 is typical of the sort of figures used. Then the quasi-canonic style of even quavers heard earlier alternates with violently detached chords in rhythmic unison of 'pleasure, ease and sloth', and the music sinks to silence. The altos now refer to 'the conquered' in the original (slower) tempo, and a quieter, more fragmentary section only gradually rises to *forte* massed chords on 'therefore cool'd in zeal.' After a fermata, the last phrase ('For the Earth shall bear more than enough . . .') is set in five-part harmony, *andante, molto semplice*. The harmonic style — strongly diatonic and centred around

Ex. 3

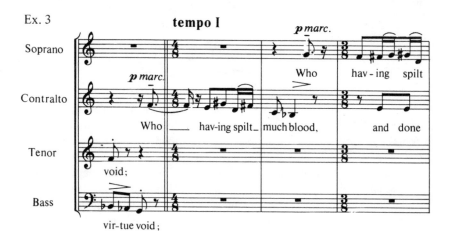

Ex. 3 cont.

A Major, which chord appears very sonorously, with an added sixth — is again not only extremely effective in context but also prophetic (as, in a different way, are the chords of Ex. 2) of the broadening of this composer's harmonic palette.

The second of these choruses is in a ternary form and it also plays off solo voices against full choir — indeed, as this also happens in the later Blake settings, Op. 17, the device might be said to be characteristic of Goehr's choral style. The opening phrase for solo alto is much enhanced (in the case

of the John Alldis Choir) by being sung by a male alto, whose distinctively
reedy tone contributes to the desired wayward, disordered effect of this
passage (Ex. 4).

Ex. 4

The alto is joined in duet by solo soprano: soon the rest of the altos settle
on a tolling third (C♯ – E♮), whilst above is heard the echoing tritone on
the word 'follows' (B♮ –F♮) that is going to play a large part in the succeeding section. The tutti voices take up the tritone and gradually build up
to a climax at 'higher than the shores,' and a bigger one, in eight parts, at the
words 'force should be right . . .' After a quieter phrase the music of this
section is rounded off briskly by 'And so should justice too' sung in peremp-
tory octaves. The solo soprano and alto then resume their intricate duet to
the words, 'Then ev'rything includes itself in pow'r' and are joined by the
choir in the closing homophonic passage of gasping detached phrases, curt
and appalled, but with sudden ominous crescendi on the words 'seconded' and
'an universal prey,' and sinking into silence with '. . . and last . . . eat up
. . . himself.'

These fine choruses are strongly contrasted one with the other in style and
effect. The first is outward, straightforward, comparatively easy to grasp and
has a vigorous rhythmic impetus; the second is (in spite of the public character of its theme) almost introverted, brooding, uncanny – and it uses a much
more intricate rhythmic vocabulary, particularly in the opening and closing
sections. But the choruses complement each other in these contrasts and in
their common atmosphere of high seriousness and mature musical utterance.

Goehr's next choral work was also written for the John Alldis Choir during the spring of 1964, in response to a commission from the City of London Festival. He returned to Blake for his text: these *Five Poems and an Epigram of William Blake* are inscribed 'For Michael Tippett's sixtieth birthday, in friendship.' Most of the poems are, in fact, so concise as to be almost epigrammatic and they are set in a way which clearly displays the pungent brevity of the thought. Both the first two ('Never seek to tell thy love' and 'I laid me down upon a bank') set a solo voice against the chorus, which echoes its leader, phrase by brief phrase. The brooding melancholy of both is well caught by the gently dissonant harmony. The third lyric is more involved: this is Blake's uncanny allegory of the 'chapel all of gold,' the serpent forcing its way in and 'Vomiting his poison out / On the bread and on the wine.' This demands more extended treatment and a wider range of contrast. The opening section is set in pure and spare counterpoint, fading away on the word 'worshipping.' The bass then begins the section 'I saw a serpent,' set in the same character but most effectively overtaken by the other voices singing the same text to shorter values, and reaching a really violent climax with the much repeated word 'forc'd'. After a fermata, the final couplet, 'So I turn'd into a sty / And laid me down among the swine,' is sung by a solo alto (the phrase is reminiscent of the beginning) joined by tenors and basses in block chords which end with a sudden intense crescendo on the words 'among the swine.'

'I asked a thief to steal me a peach: / He turn'd up his eyes.' The contrast, in this sarcastic fable, between the poet's lack of success in immoral doings and the angel's paradoxical freedom from the moral code, is enhanced by the sustained rhetorical recitative-like nature of the first half and the rapid *scherzando leggiero* of the second. The epigram 'The sword sang on the barren heath' is a four-line verse, first heard in octaves from the whole choir, then as a simple canon at the octave, in this order of voices: soprano, tenor, bass, alto. As each voice ceases after completing the four lines, the alto is left on its own at the end. A trumpet in D is added to the choir for the last piece. The first phrase, 'I heard an Angel singing . . . .' is sung to a pedal B, later D on the trumpet, then, as it leaps up to F, the words 'Mercy, Pity, Peace /Is the world's release' are sung like a chorale, with mainly triadic harmonies in which the triad of B Minor is prominent. 'I heard a Devil curse . . .' returns to the opening material: pedal B then F on the trumpet, but this time with a frenetic accession of violence (spoken voice in the soprano part) on the words 'devil's curse' and a very high trill on the trumpet. Then the Devil's perversion of the Angel's song is again sung like a chorale, with the key of B Minor even more prominent, but against more agitated arpeggios on the trumpet. Left on its own, the trumpet sinks to an ostinato figure, and is overtaken by the re-entry of the choir rising to the final climax and quiet ending, stressing the ironic moral: 'And Miseries' increase/Is Mercy, Pity, Peace.'

The Blake songs are on a smaller scale than the Op. 14 Choruses, and, it may be felt, not so distinctive in musical character as the earlier work. But the last of them, the most sustained of the set, contains some notable invention and makes a deep impression.

Why Must Arden Die?

DAVID DREW

Arden Must Die — 'an opera on the death of the wealthy Arden of Faversham' with music by Alexander Goehr and libretto by Erich Fried — was commissioned by the Hamburg State Opera; enthusiastically applauded by the majority of the audience at the first night on 4th March 1967; and opposed by a small, and perhaps organized, minority. 'It seems,' wrote the critic of *Die Welt* two days after the première, 'that only a part of the public really understood the intellectual fascination of the music and the production. It would be interesting if an open discussion were to disclose exactly why young members of the audience protested against the composer and librettist'. Such a discussion would, of course, have been profoundly irrelevant unless conducted on the clear understanding that whatever the 'young members of the audience' were bothered about, *Arden Must Die* will, or will not, survive on the strength of its music. It is an opera, not a 'musicalized play'— to use a Broadway term appropriate to pseudo-operas that achieve ephemeral success by parading a more-or-less shapely play in some kind of musical negligée.

The opposition to *Arden* was not quite as *Die Welt* and other papers have described it. The dissenters, whether acting on impulse or instructions, made themselves far more audible when the composer and author took their bows together than when the composer reappeared on his own. But although Fried is a controversial figure in both parts of Germany, it was surely not his already publicized position that caused the Hamburg uproar. It was the content, or at any rate the finally manifest tendency, of the libretto. And for that, of course, the composer is also responsible. If he has indeed written a real opera, then the music forms the libretto and is informed by it. To ask what the protests were about should be a way of asking what the music is about.

In the Hamburg programme-notes, Goehr described *Arden* thus: 'an opera about men and the manner in which they treat their fellow-men; hence a political opera about ourselves and the way we behave in the crises in which we are involved'. A political opera: already the bulls begin to snort, though what they take for a red rag may yet prove to be a red herring. From Sarastro's sacred halls through Pizarro's prison to Wotan's Valhalla and Wozzeck's barrack-room, the path of opera has repeatedly crossed political and social territory. To what extent, if any, are the politics of *Arden* different from those which are long familiar in the opera house?

The material is derived from the anonymous 16th-century play, *Arden of Faversham,* and from Holinshed. The wealthy and avaricious Arden is done to death through the combined efforts of his wife Alice and her lover, Mosbie, who are in league with his servants, and with Greene and Reede, two land-owners whom he has ruined. Mrs. Bradshaw, a neighbour, is party to the plot but remains, in her submission, a helpless onlooker.

Black Will and Shakebag, the two professional cut-throats hired by Arden's enemies to do their dirty work, prove incompetent. They plan to murder Arden as he crosses the marshes on a business trip to London (the ferry-boat scene). But they lose their way in the fog, and the plan misfires. So do its two successors. Finally they succeed in their mission, but only because Arden has rashly invited his 'friends' to a reconciliation banquet. The Mayor and his constables – with Mrs. Bradshaw's help – discover the body and hold a summary trial. Alice and Mosbie admit their guilt, the others make excuses and quarrel among themselves, the cut-throats offer their sevices as hangmen (which the Mayor seems inclined to accept), and lastly, Mrs. Bradshaw turns King's evidence. The Mayor and constables hail her example as proof that wrong-doers can 'surmount the past' if they are truly repentant. With that, the drama ends; the spoken epilogue (set as melodrama) has now been omitted.

Up to the trial scene, the plot roughly follows that of the 16th-century play – though necessarily by a much swifter route. The various motives for the murder, as set out in the opening scene, are similar to those of the original characters. The differences are of tone and tendency. *Arden of Faversham* is a domestic tragedy about frail mortals, and its closing message is religious: the wages of sin is death, but the Saviour is at hand. *Arden Must Die* is a morality play in the modern secular tradition of Epic Theatre (without 'psychology' or moral conflict), and its final picture is as black as the first. The only decent character, Franklin, is a cypher. The only honest ones, in the sense that they conceal nothing, are the cut-throats. In short, an 'opera about men' con-ceived exclusively in terms of the negative example. Arden's death, so long struggled for and so messily achieved, is, in itself, entirely without tragic implications: for the mode of life Arden has hitherto represented is plainly worthless. Until the final scene, this seems to be the crux of the drama. It proves an awkward one.

In *Arden of Faversham,* Greene says of Arden:

> Desire of wealth is endless in his mind,
> And he is greedy-gaping still for gain.

Greene is not being altogether fair. The play's Arden is indeed 'greedy-gaping'. But next to, if not above, his desire for wealth is his love of Alice; and it is that love which inspires his last effort to make peace with Mosbie and lends a certain tragic dignity to his otherwise murky end. In *Arden Must Die,* his love for Alice is reduced to insignificance – as it had to be, given the dialectics of the Epic Theatre. The gesture of reconciliation thus becomes another of Arden's characteristic absurdities – in this case a sentimental one. The centuries that separate him from his prototype are most evident at the banquet, when he invites Reede and Greene to rejoice in his good fortune, and adds: 'That is the holy rule of free enterprise, which makes one rich and the other poorer'.

If this is what a post-Marxian Arden stands for – and such was unquestionably the emphasis in the excellent Hamburg production* – then his death acquires an ideological significance quite distinct from the various local expediencies that led to it. As a bumbling representative of (shall we say?) bourgeois individualistic competitiveness, Arden would seem to have been conceived and reared for the purposes of slaughter. Clearly, Fried and Goehr are principals in the plot to do away with him; and whether their chosen title is a categorical imperative or merely a statement of the inevitable, they certainly do not ask us to bewail his demise. What conclusions are we encouraged to draw from it?

Immediately before the murder of Arden, Susan sings a lute-song, *Am Weg so rot die Rose glüht'* (on the road so red the roses glow); after it, the song becomes a triumphal duet for Alice and Mosbie. In his 1967 programme-note, Fried observed that the text is a paraphrase of the song *'Am Weg die rote Rose blüht, wenn die SA nach Moskau zieht'.* So far from shedding light on the murder, the references would envelope it in a fog as thick as the one that saved Arden from an earlier death were it not so esoteric as to be undetectable without the gloss. Goehr wisely pretends to ignore it, and sets the words at their bloodstained face-value. So when the Mayor cries 'Open up! In the name of the law!' the crucial question remains: whose law? If the answer is the same as in the original play, the murder will at last acquire a clear moral context; but only at the expense of its (unclear) ideological one. If on the other hand it is the law enunciated by Arden at the banquet, the main concern will be the preservation of the socio-economic *status quo,* and discussion of such questions as political murder or genocide will become difficult.

Not surprisingly, the Court scene seems to be in two or three minds about who and what is on trial. In the first part, the Mayor and his entourage apply the universal standards and can be accepted as universally typical despite or because of their tendency to indulge in self-righteous moralizing. But then

* Directed by Egon Monk, from the school of Brecht, and designed by Ekkehard Grübler, from the school of Neher. The Arden (Toni Blankenheim) was to some extent a cross between Brecht's Pierpont Mauler and Puntila; and Mosbie (Ronald Dowd) verged on the Berliner Ensemble's recently reconstructed Macheath; Greene and Reede, grotesquely unwilling recruits to the Lumpenproletariat, were like severed halves of Filch, or the Fewkombey of the *Der Dreigroschenroman;* and the organ-pipe motif in the settings was derived from Neher's original sets for *Die Dreigroschenoper,* but sensibly developed as a mechanical exit-and-entry device in accordance with the deterministic structure of the libretto.

Greene and Reede start ranting about the *arme Leute,* and the Mayor calls the hangmen in. Instantly the whole picture changes. The cut-throats offer their services to the Mayor; the Mayor responds in a manner that deprives him of all claim to moral authority; and the shadows of Adenauer's Germany, as seen by its critics, fall across the stage. A sense that the authors, like Black Will and Shakebag, had at last fulfilled their mission was apparently confirmed at Hamburg by the challenge with which Fried ended his programme-note: 'He who feels himself insulted is the one who is meant'. One sees why the critic of *Die Welt* was puzzled by the fact that *young* people were among those who protested — though the *NPD* press office would have had a ready explanation. Yet Fried's parting shot may still leave us wondering whether all those who are 'meant' really will be 'insulted', or indeed (if the distinction is allowable) whether those who are meant to be insulted really will be.

The spoken epilogue (which now survives only in the published libretto) was ironically apologetic. In the first two verses, the audience was reminded — as it needed to be — of the original dramatic situation (and of its historical authenticity). But in the third and last verse it was jerked back into the world of the trial scene (and hence of the *Deutsche National-Zeitung,* whose front-page headline on 3 March 1967 ran, *Wieviele Juden wurden wirklich ermordet? Sechs Millionen-Lüge endgültig zusammengebrochen):*

> But with one thing you can console yourselves as you go off home:
>> you yourselves
> Are not guilty of murder or indeed of any other crime:
> Neither miscreants nor accessories, nor people who would rather
>> not know,
> And even if you were, you are not like Alice in her own four walls,
> But far further off and much better organised.

Indeed they are not like Alice. That is the trouble.

The spoken words were accompanied, as if from a great distance, by isolated *espressivo* phrases whose lyricism was as ambiguous as that of Eisler's score for *Nuit et Brouillard.* The whispers of a music that appears to be looking the other way somehow carried further than the text's half-smothered shout of *J'accuse!;* and they made further indictments superfluous.

If anything was achieved by the noisy few who demonstrated against the opera at its Hamburg première, it was to over-expose the authors' forgivable uncertainty about the extent of their involvement with a German audience. Largely because the 'responsible' press kept away from, or floated above, the political questions, the demonstrators' case was never examined, and *Arden* was allowed to become an object of mute and irrelevant embarrassment — with results that were likely to affect its future.

Fortunately, its artistic stature remains unimpaired by such considerations. From that point of view, the political aim is of less concern than the structural problem inherent in the general argumentation. The thesis — about Arden — and the antithesis — about the murderers — are both negative and are not easily and comprehensibly amenable to the kind of broad synthesis opera hankers after.

However, some of the difficulties are overcome by the recurrent Bradshaw-motif, which is Fried's and Goehr's own invention, and a brilliant one. The irony of Mrs. Bradshaw's triumphant rehabilitation is consistent with the anti-bourgeois theme and comprehensible without reference to contemporary politics (though the Mayor's homily about 'surmounting the past' allows for such a reference). It is the music which raises the irony to the level of social tragedy, by reminding us, thematically, of the truth about Mrs. Bradshaw. She, we hear, and hear more clearly than if the idea were expressed in words, is the chief culprit. This is what the music has been 'about' since the musically unforgettable moment in the first scene when Mrs. Bradshaw foresees her vindication on the Day of Judgment.

Since the music is more concerned with the characterization of attitudes than with the direct expression of the text — and so defines the epic style of the whole work — the tempo as well as the tone is fundamentally different from that of traditional romantic or neo-romantic opera. The way in which Goehr tends to establish connections and draw analogies between the characters, by means of variation, rather than differentiate between them, by means of traditional dramatic contrast, is clearly illustrated by the music of scene 2. Arden appears for the first time and makes two characteristic statements: first that his business affairs are prospering, second that his wife is unfaithful. Musically, both statements occur within the same harmonic field and have the same 'expressive' weight. That music, one might suppose, is Arden's personal property. But it is immediately transferred to Alice as she congratulates her husband on his good fortune (which is soon, she hopes, to become all her own). It remains her music while she acts the rôle of a faithful and loving wife. After Arden's departure, Alice is re-united with her lover. Their 'love' music is an enriched and heightened variation of the Arden music — enriched texturally and heightened tonally in a dominant direction. The lyrical foliage makes a splendid show; which is to say, it is pure décor, as we would expect. Sure enough, Alice and Mosbie's thoughts turn from love to murder — both gainful — just as Arden's had turned from business to love. So the musical continuity has established the idea of property as the middle term in a syllogism about love and sensuality: *Geld macht sinnlich,* as they would say in *Mahagonny.*

Clearly, Goehr intends the 'love' music, whatever it represents, to be sensuously enjoyable: and so it is (not least because it cunningly reinvests a part of Janáček's legacy). Likewise, the elegiac tone of the music for the memorial tributes uttered by the delighted conspirators when a shepherd tells them that Arden has met his death on the marshes somehow conveys a touching regret at the absence of genuine feeling. The dramatic situation is pure *Volpone,* or rather, *Gianni Schicchi.* The music goes its own way. An immensely droll effect is achieved with an 11-bar chorale whose asymmetrical structure exposes the conflict between the conspirators' real and pretended emotions: the latter holding sway for three precariously balanced three-bar phrases, the former implied by a too-sudden and altogether vicious cadence. The point is reinforced, not weakened, by repetition. Indeed the timing of the whole scene after the premature announcement of Arden's death is masterly. The conspirators go through each of their motions of grief once too often, and that once is just right.

The dramatic rightness of so many things in the score is astonishing. Sometimes it is a question of imagery – for instance, the fantastic Messiaen-like effulgence of Arden's invitation to the banquet, or the whole complex of aqueous and vaporous ideas in the ferry-boat scene. But such local successes would be of little account without the larger insights. Musico-dramatically, the total form is successful to so great an extent that it is hard to credit the fact that this is Goehr's first opera. That the challenge for Goehr was one of genuine dramatic expression is revealed by the least convincing section in the score. Although the long first scene in Act II has many good things in it, the general effect is episodic. This reflects a similar weakness in the libretto – indeed, the only weakness of that kind. Dramatically, there is no decisive event between Arden's proposal of a reconciliation banquet, at the end of Act I, and the banquet itself.

Besides mastering many aspects of dramatic form, Goehr has almost solved a technical problem that has defeated numerous modern opera composers, including those who are most experienced and more fluent than he: the problem of finding a declamatory style sufficiently flexible for the various demands made upon it, while preserving some degree of orchestral autonomy. This is not only a question of technique but also of idiom. Its solution must have been all the more difficult in the case of *Arden,* because the idiom implied by the libretto and its regular strophic form is at odds with the preoccupations of most contemporary composers, Goehr among them. The collapse of tonality as a governing principle, and the complexity or complication of the devices replacing it, have deprived the modern opera composer of a convenient means of distinguishing between salient and secondary events, between what is essential to the drama and what is required merely in order to sustain its continuity. The forms of traditional recitative can be imitated; but their function is lost if, as is so often the case in modern operas, the harmonic density and the general rate of progress is too great.

The spirit of compromise in which Goehr seems to have composed *Arden* is wholly positive. It enabled him to write his most direct and yet various score till then; and so far from costing him something of his individuality it notably added to it. Having accepted opera's traditional priorities, he found his own tonal and rhythmic devices for expressing the dramatic shifts of pace and emphasis; and having granted the importance of the words, he evolved voice-and-accompaniment textures that are often models of their kind. In the organisation of pitch, and other elements, he establishes a wide field and then selects or introduces narrower ones. The areas of static tonal harmony within a fluid non-tonal boundary correspond to the areas of ostinato rhythm or quasi-symmetrical phrasing within those that are relatively or extremely loose in definition.

The musical style, like the technique, is outwardly heterogeneous and inwardly consistent. In principle it owes much to Goehr's teacher, Messiaen, though in sound the resemblances are few. It is not difficult to identify Goehr's sources; but neither is it particularly helpful. Some critical confusion about the work's style seems to have been caused by Fried's ill-advised reference to parody — ill-advised only because the whole subject of operatic parody has been bedevilled by Brecht's *Anmerkungen zur Oper,* a fascinating exercise in self-justification whose objective value the Germans, and not only they, tend to overrate. Fried did not, of course, mean that *Arden* is some kind of persiflage, though the idea might recommend itself to those who insist on regarding Weill's *Mahagonny* or even Stravinsky's *Rake* in those terms.

Not the least intelligent thing Goehr has done, however, is to bypass Stravinsky and Weill. In their different ways both composers offered ready-made solutions for a libretto of this kind, and such solutions — even assuming that these particular ones would be artistically renewable today — have never attracted Goehr. There is a certain tough independence about his musical personality. One can see from his earliest works, indeed from his Op. 2 Piano Sonata, that it is native to him. But it has grown with his own increasing awareness that in his work every real advance means fighting, inch by inch, for things which are often 'given' to others. In consequence his development, though remarkably steady and consistent, has never been of the sort to create journalistic sensations. (It would do so if the chronology of his works could be telescoped so that, say, the Op. 4 Fantasia for orchestra stood next to the Op. 19 *Pastorals,* or the Op. 10 cantata *Sutter's Gold* next to *Arden*). His reward is that whatever he wins for himself has acquired in the process of being won a kind of urgency and authenticity lacking from the work of composers to whom equivalent ideas may come without effort. There are pages in *Arden* which get as close to the heart of the matter as anything in the multifarious stage-works of Hans Werner Henze, to cite a similarly eclectic composer of approximately the same generation but of very different creative temperament. Although there are some striking parallels between Goehr's *Arden* and Henze's *The Bassarids,* they went unnoticed by the German critics. It is not altogether surprising, for the parallels are far apart and not co-extensive. But between them runs the plausible part of Auden's famous half-truth about librettos.

Auden, we recall, declared that, 'the verses which the librettist writes are not addressed to the public but are really a private letter to the composer'. A libretto like Fried's, which on one side is certainly addressed to the public, arrives in the first instance by registered post and must at that moment be checked. But sooner or later the public changes its address, and the urgent messages of today return to the sorting-office and become the dead letters of tomorrow: unless, that is, they contain other observations about which there was no particular hurry, because they are always true. If *Arden*, or for that matter, *The Bassarids*, is to live, it will be because of such observations and the response they have elicited from the composer. While the death of Arden already seems an inept symbol of the crimes characteristic of our age or society, the survival of Mrs. Bradshaw, to whom we are all related, is part of an ageless story.

Notes on Goehr's Triptych

MELANIE DAIKEN

Goehr sub-titled his *Shadowplay* 'Music theatre'. This is what *Naboth's Vineyard* and *Sonata about Jerusalem* are also usually called. Yet what is music theatre? It seems it can be a monodrama like *Pierrot Lunaire* or a panto-mimic, 'dramatic pastoral' like Birtwistle's *Down by the Greenwood Side*. It can be a set of musical tableaux linked by spoken passages like *The Soldier's Tale* or a free interpretation by mime of vocal and percussive sounds like Ligeti's *Nouvelles Aventures*.

It is easier to explain what music theatre is not, than to define what it is. It is certainly not 'poor' opera, and in the case of *Triptych*, Goehr was not interested in opera and all its paraphernalia – too long to compose and too indirect for what he wanted to put over. A small ensemble of singers and players, a producer, designer and an actor/mime or two can be enough. The composer provides the music and some of his own background imagery and then collaborates with the team. Though the score is fixed, a new dramatic interpretation may result every time.

The works were written quickly. Each lasts well under 30 minutes. I first saw *Triptych* in 1971 at the Brighton Festival in the Music Theatre Ensemble productions of John Cox conducted by Goehr himself. These three rare works stirred me. Fragile, yet they seemed to offer such resistance. I thought – they will survive.

Goehr turns to age-old classical and biblical subjects for his vocal works: *The Deluge, Virtues,* the Two Choruses. Or proverbial texts, allegories and parables, as in his Blake settings. He is pre-occupied with human suffering and oppression and with 'Mercy, Pity, Peace'. The subjects of *Triptych* are universal; timeless like legends and fairy tales. Children can understand them.

Naboth's Vineyard is a parable from Kings I. Goehr's presentation appears on the surface neutral, ritualised as it is in the style of the Japanese Nō theatre or the Renaissance dramatic madrigal. It has none of the black humour of *Arden Must Die,* though it can be produced in such a way that the existing humour is brought out. The musical style is more homogeneous than *Arden,* the protagonists depersonalised, the singers used for commentary like a Greek chorus. This is not emotive opera where we identify with the pro-

Alexander Goehr   (Laelia Goehr)

Arden Muss Sterben, Hamburg State Opera 1967. Alice (Kerstin Meyer), Arden (Toni Blankenheimer), Mosbie (Ronald Dowd), Black Bill, about to jump (Manfred Schenk), Shakebag (Kurt Marschner) (Peyer)

Naboth's Vineyard, performed by the Music Theatre Ensemble

(Laelia Goehr)

Before *The Deluge*: Alexander Goehr lecturing at the ICA, 1959

(Laelia Goehr)

tagonist. Goehr takes his stand from a distance and 'shoots' like Eisenstein, close, profile, telescopically. But this 'abstract' approach should not be mistaken for coolness. The works are heavily committed.

Naboth is about the killing of a man (Naboth) in the name of a king (Achab) through the intrigue of a queen (Jezebel) in order to gain a piece of property. It is a story of avarice, repentance, retribution. There are two sides to the dramatic coin: Jezebel's persuasion tactics could be funny; Achab's being thrown out of the vineyard is sheer Buster Keaton humour. It was reading a similar incident in Gilchrist's *Life of William Blake* that suggested the story to Goehr in the first place: the angry poet lifting a soldier he suspected of making advances to his wife out of his Shoreham garden *by the elbows*. But the subsequent summoning of Blake to Chichester Assizes on a charge of sedition was serious. And Elijah's admonition to Achab is serious. And Jezebel's 'lapidatus eum' is deadly serious.

The scoring is for contralto, tenor and bass, flute/piccolo/alto flute, clarinet/bass clarinet, bass trombone, violin, double bass and piano four-hands. Together the singers constitute the chorus while individually they sing the four rôles in the story (the bass doubles Naboth and Elijah). The tenor is an arrogant, peevish Achab, for instance, who constantly asserts himself (like the plutocrat in St Exupéry's *Petit Prince*). The characters sing and speak in Latin with plainchant-like melismata. The chorus narrate in English. This setting of the characters at a certain remove matches their enactment by a pair of mimes wearing interchangeable masks.

Mime is a powerfully expressive medium. Unlike the dancer, the mime can add a dimension without duplication: he can describe by symbolism, by contradiction and obliquely by cross-reference — his chief rehearsal guide, the stopwatch. Masks have a long tradition in both Western and Eastern theatre. In the council scene, Jezebel's alternation of a double mask showing on one side the bland elders, on the other, the malicious Sons of Belial vividly suggests Naboth's confusion at his false trial. This was particularly successful in John Cox's original production.

The work is in two halves: it seems to reach peak tension at the stoning of Naboth, then a hiatus; then in the second half comes the judgement, building-up slowly, deliberately, with long melismas from the bass as Elijah. Within this scheme, the instrumental contribution varies from the little set-piece march to which Achab enters with heavy gait — processional, like a train of camels, weighted down with power — to the brilliant solo clarinet 'sketching-in' of Jezebel — Ex. 1.

After Achab's march and Jezebel's exhortation, the action — and the evil — mount almost automatically to the stoning. Scene 4, in which Jezebel

Ex.1

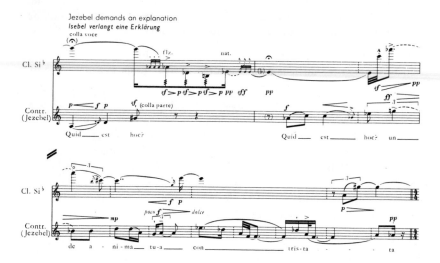

summons the elders, denounces Naboth and has him stoned is a striking example of how music theatre can fuse into a single event a sequence that might require several scenes in an opera. Thus: Chorus, 'She writes letters in Achab's name' — imitation by high instruments (piccolo and clarinet) of the tenor and bass, so that the writing is done *by her* (high) but *in his name* (low), while repeated violin notes attack and follow through in a marvellous way the scraping pen. The music then underlines the reversing of the double mask in rapid switches of texture. The stoning is done without singing, by mime and instruments alone. The bass trombone represents the voice of Naboth while the other instruments create a series of onslaughts which grow in ferocity against it. Its last breath — then a single stroke of the tamtam. So ends the first half.

Stillness. The Lord comes to Elijah — deliberate, chorale-like. Achab pretends not to see him but is forced to bow down and ask forgiveness (the march theme again in a new variant). The face-to-face stroke of doom is delivered with terrible finality. Achab is spared for now, but "In his son's days I will bring calamity on all his house". We are left in a void. Do we reject Achab or pity him? Or do we blame it all on the fault of the system that there should be potentates at all? And do we think of historical parallels nearer our own time — between the fate of the unyielding Naboth, perhaps, and that of the mighty firm of Krupp in Hitler Germany?

Shadowplay is different. A poetic music drama, its subject is taken from Plato's *Republic*. This is projected on three levels: narration (tenor, singing a direct translation of Plato), enactment (the prisoner, speaking a more ornate monologue by Kenneth Cavender) and dramatic articulation and evocation (the instrumental score).

A man is shackled with others in a dark cave. Behind burns a fire and in front stretches a high wall. The man interprets the shadows thrown against the wall as reality. He is freed and makes a tortuous ascent through the unknown towards the light, wanting at the same time the world he is leaving. He sees the sun and moon as they really are and watches the seasons and all the beauty of the earth. He is dazzled.... but then, is there a way back? Would he not be blinded in reverse by the darkness of the cave, and his companions, if he tried to free them, would they not mock him or even kill him?

Goehr's musical structure and evocative surface are indissolubly one with the arch-shape of the allegory. Dry, understated recitative sets the scene. Intermezzo I evokes the flickering fire in repeated notes. The recitative becomes fiercer as the Prisoner's head is released and he looks directly at the fire — horn stopped and unstopped (moan), reiterated piano and wind (wrenching). Intermezzo II (ensemble) — the Prisoner scrambling up to the light. His discovery of the world — his own hand, trees, the waterpool, sky, clouds, moon and rising sun — at once a set of variations on Intermezzo II and a cumulative tone poem. The tenor enters controlling the beat and counterpointed by the saxophone in long lyrical phrases over murmuring melismata of great delicacy and sustained emotional effect — expressing far deeper than words the world of the spirit. Climactic apotheosis of the seasons — exalted rhetoric. Intermezzo III — return towards the dark, jagged phrases, fugitive, *sul ponticello* cello, dungeon sounds. Dry, understated recitative for denouncement.

Shadowplay is fine music, probably some of Goehr's best. I feel he has broken into a type of expression new to him. It is scored for tenor, alto flute, alto saxophone, horn, cello and piano, a sensuous combination. Goehr's notation develops constantly and is always geared to time-saving in rehearsal and flexibility in performance. In the central tone poem, configurations of notes, randomly permutated and released according to a set of cues, create an effect which could not otherwise be assured. They can be prolonged, their dynamics varied, and co-ordinated with the action on stage. The conductor usually gives the beat, but here the piano can be led by the tenor and saxophone — Ex. 2.

I have witnessed three productions of *Shadowplay*. 1) a literal dramatisation showing fire and bodies for what they are. 2) an idea culled from the Princeton experiments where a man was isolated from all external stimuli, to

Ex. 2

see how he reacted. 3) a television production with film-strip of flames, sun etc., substituting for real stage effects. None of them, to my mind, did the work justice. The latent problem is the danger of triplication. To say, 'Imagine a hollowed out chamber', then to describe it in music, then to show it on stage, is too much. The work was transfigured by the Princeton experiment production, but this was grafted on to the original. Ideas for analogies: the ascent could be interpreted as a fairytale of a man groping his way through a forest towards the light, or set like Beckett's *Les Depeupleurs* in a closed rubber cylinder.

In *Sonata about Jerusalem,* music and theatre are held in unforced, effective balance. Goehr appears to have had Monteverdi's *Sonata sopra Sancta Maria* in mind as his musical model, in which the dominating feature is the refrain − giving it a more rondo-like character to post-classical ears. The Latin words of Goehr's refrain − 'The sun shall turn into darkness and the moon into blood before the great and terrible day of the Lord' − are derived from the autobiography of Obadiah the Proselyte, an Italian monk from Oppidou who became a convert to Judaism and fled to the East where he travelled and observed Jewish communities in Jerusalem, Syria and Persia. The other source of the libretto is the Chronicle of Samuel ben Yahya ben al Maghribi and the work is dedicated to Mrs. Recha Freier who helped Goehr arrange the words and was instrumental in the commissioning of the score by Testimonium, Jerusalem, in 1971.

The story runs as follows: the Jews of 12th century Baghdad, subjugated and tormented, are brought news by a mad girl of a false messiah who will rescue them and lead them back to Jerusalem. The wisest of the Jews don green clothing, the colour of paradise, climb to the roofs of their houses and await a miracle. As night falls, they see a vision of Jerusalem. In their ecstasy, they seem to become a great bird − they fly. But the morning finds them still on their rooftops. They descend among the jeering crowd and a child mocks them.

The musico-dramatic distribution results in genuinely functional complements. Sometimes the music holds sway as in the rejoicing of the Jews, the donning of the robes, the nocturnal changing of the light and vision of paradise. Sometimes words call the tune, with mimes and instruments equally 'acting out' the ideas. Sometimes the mimes are activated, highlighted by the music and allowed to steal the show. Here the music may suggest the manner of miming (as in the processional trombone solo for the High Governor of Baghdad), or a context against which the mimes can react (as in the Mad Girl scene) or an 'objective correlative' (as in the music for the beating of the Jews). Whatever of theatre is enclosed by the music, it is never eclipsed by it. And where theatre leads (and there is plenty of scope for spectacle and buffoonery) the piece remains a tight musical structure with the refrain giving the whole its pace and onwardness.

Music theatre is nothing new to the Israelis. Generations of Jewish children have dressed up, danced and clowned to biblical stories and stories of their

own invention at the festivals of Hannukah and Purim. *Sonata about Jerusalem*
was first performed in its original Hebrew text (the published version is in
English) at Tel-Aviv and Jerusalem in January 1971. It is striking how its
sound and character seems to draw upon Hebraic culture both old and new,
religious and secular.

The archaic band sound of the instrumental writing – a kind of high,
bright, rhetorical heterophony – apparently derives from Goehr's search for
equivalents within his own resources to ancient instruments. Piccolo and
clarinet suggest the ûgãbh (vertical pipe); high, agile B flat trumpet writing,
the hazozerah (metal trumpet) – Ex. 3 (a). Pungent combinations of wind
and strings give the reedy effect of the halîl (double oboe). Trombone
glissandi evoke the shophar (ram's or goat's horn). Piano and pizzicato strings
suggest the plucked kinnôr (lyre) and rehbel (harp or psaltery) – Ex. 3 (b) –
and piano tremoli, the thrummings of the měnnaaním (sistrum).

Hebrew and Roman styles of chant are closely related. The Latin refrain of
the work takes a Gregorian, three-part form. Equally, much of the vocal
writing seems to imitate the Jewish style of cantillation upon ancient chants
from the liturgy of the wandering, post-biblical Jews – Ex. 3 (c). There are
hints, too, of other ritual styles brought to Judaism through Sumeric culture:
the alalu (shouts of joy) – Ex. 3 (d) – and the eršemma (psalm of lamentation)
– Ex. 3 (e). The sounds and words of the original Hebrew text of the work,
its stresses and inflections, also seem to have shaped Goehr's rhythmic style –
its syllabic accents, decorations, repeated notes and dance patterns. These, in
turn, have seeded a special form of accompaniment in which instruments spit
out heads of phrases, light off-beat sparks, burgeon into melismas and recoil
into punctuations.

Instrumental colour, chant, linguistics: all these seem evident influences.
But they may not be entirely conscious ones. Goehr apparently made no very
systematic study of such sources before embarking on the work. It is often
difficult to separate the intrinsic characteristics of Goehr's technique from the
influences he invokes. His own highly developed serial-modal language quite
naturally encompasses and develops the ancient Hebraic chant – its propensity for contour variation and melismatic decoration. In the same way his
instrumental writing shows strong affinities with the 'central European'
sounds of some of his other scores: plucked banjo timbres, gypsy sounds,
Vienna, the double stops of Jewish fiddle style, the folk band with its violent
dynamics, glissandi, pizzicato, hiss, *cuivre.*

But the context of the *Sonata about Jerusalem* seems to have liberated
such correspondences with particular vividness. At some points sheer sound
reigns: shimmering night sounds for the changing of the light – melismas
around one note, deliciously gauged timbres of violin *poco articulato*, flute

Ex. 3
(a)

and cello harmonics, clarinet *pppp* (echo tone), piano trilling. A muted trumpet heralds the flight attempt. Illustration seems to take over but as the 'flight' veers towards the impending refrain, we hear that colour and structure are indissolubly welded — the mad girl and her fey lyricism, stuttering, unhinged; the beating of the Jews; the Yiddish type of lament; the child's mocking at the end. And repeated notes — almost a Goehr thumbprint — run through the *Triptych:* in *Naboth* evoking Japanese Nō woodblocks or Jezebel's scratching pen; in *Shadowplay,* the flickering of the light. *Sonata about Jerusalem* shows almost a score of usages. Repeated notes here create ostinati and build-ups, invoke ecstasy, lyricism, dance, clarify cadence and speech contours, suggest stuttering and sobbing.

The inward vision of the *Triptych* is something apart from the outward drama, yet the outward takes its form from the inward in this music theatre that Goehr has made his own.

The Chamber Music

PETER-PAUL NASH

Compared with the continuous evolution suggested by Alexander Goehr's thirteen orchestral works so far produced, the eight pieces (excluding the unpublished String Quartet No. 1, 1956-7) that can broadly be identified as chamber music might appear to comprise a more intermittent sequence. There is, for instance, nothing from the years 1962-65, when Goehr was first developing his methods of serial modality. However, such gaps could be seen to emphasise the emergence and operation of a kind of triangular tension between the properties of Goehr's own technique, his invocation of a variety of stylistic surfaces from other music and his use of works from the past as formal models – and the way the particular character of each work is affected by the degree to which these concerns work together or against one another.

If the Piano Trio, Op. 20 (1966), offers the most striking example of a working together, this is surely because its stylistic surface and formal procedures derive from a common source that also offers close analogies to Goehr's own processes. The folkloristic provenance of the throaty tone, jagged phrasing, glissandi and double stopping is immediately obvious in the opening statement of Ex. 1 or, perhaps more specifically, a tradition of dealing with such material, since Goehr's use of clusters, percussive low notes and other gestural devices not only suggest Bartókian affinities in general, but clear parallels with such pieces as the third of Bartók's *Three Rondos on Folk Tunes* – Ex. 2. Here, the quasi-ostinato of bars 1-5 acts as the principal refrain throughout the rondo. It is followed by a statement and varied re-statement of the single-phrase folk-melody, and a regular pattern of alternation between refrain and variation or re-statement of the melody is established, with the occasional little development interposed. Each recurrence of the melody is characterised by its individual accompaniment, based upon a single feature of the melody itself. The family resemblance with Goehr's first movement includes both its distinction in the rôle of accompaniment and its formal shape. To begin with, there is the four-square layout of material as illustrated in Ex. 1: a six-bar melody for strings, repeated; a declamatory piano solo of proportionally related length, also repeated; then varied re-statements of the opening string and piano sections, superimposing the accumulated gestural material in contrasted ways. The whole shape is confirmed by a reprise, and four variations follow, the repeat patterns kept more-or-less intact. Between the second and third variations there is a further varied statement of the opening material, the first part, corresponding to the string statement, repeated. Thus the listener's general impression of the string statement is that of both theme and refrain of the first movement as a whole.

This is not to suggest any decisive new influence for Goehr in the folk-derivation but rather to point to a fruitful coinciding of interests between the

Ex. 1.

Ex. 1 cont.

Ex. 2

exploration of the folk-origins of chamber music and the continuing development, *per se,* of well-established patterns in Goehr's treatment of serial
modality. It can be argued that the matrix system first developed in the Two
Choruses, Op. 14, tended towards a systematic exploitation of the special,
limited, and therefore individual properties of a chosen dodecaphonic set. But
the origins of such a system in the combinatorial thinking central to Goehr's
musical personality, and the resulting emphasis upon the harmonic identity of
his material simultaneously imply a certain negative resistance to harmonic

and rhythmic mobility and flow. Ironically, at least part of the success of the Trio arises from the indulgence of precisely this negative propensity. Each patch of material has its tight and enclosed rhetoric, with a balance of tension kept with its neighbours; thus a quasi-dramatic pattern of anticipation is set up leading from one section to another, but never fulfilled. Emphasis is added by the rising inflexions at the close of most sections. The parallel with the overt drama of *Sonata about Jerusalem* is particularly close: expectation from scene to scene, eventually disappointed and underlined by the unchanging refrain. However, the pattern in the Trio is intensified by the slow movement with its extreme demands upon the concentration of player and listener, its silences and pre-echo, in the coda, of a possible, but non-existent finale. This type of anticipatory conclusion is also to be found in the String Quartet No. 2 (1967) and, on a different level, in the *Concerto for Eleven* (1970), where the movement structure — a deliberate analogy with Beethoven's Piano Sonata in A major, Op. 101 — leads one to expect fulfilment in a finale, which, however, turns out to be just a reprise of first material.

Anticipatory patterns are further underlined in the Trio by a clear use of alternative pedal notes, amounting almost to an equivalent of tonic and dominant in tonality. In the first movement, every section, except the last, implies a progression analogous to that of tonic to dominant, either as an actual shift of emphasis from one pedal to another, or as a feeling within the establishment of a single pedal, such as that of the 'tonic' A♭ – G♯ in the opening string and piano statements (up to fig. 2 in Ex. 1). Each of these statements opens with the interlocking triadic structure ('a' in Ex. 3) in which both principal pedal notes are present as roots — a tone apart — of their respective major and minor triads. A♭ is given special prominence, however, by its central position in the texture and the colour of the tuned-up open G string, while the 'dominant' is placed 'en dehors' with a touch of typical grotesquerie. Both statements also conclude with another such structure ('b' in Ex. 3) with roots a tritone apart: each triadic structure retains the same harmonic sense when inverted since each mode of triad is, of course, the literal inversion of the other — there is a particularly clear instance at the beginning of the final section (fig. 19) with the inversion of the opening piano material. These are among some of the more audible triadic relationships in the movement illustrated in Ex. 3. Shift of emphasis towards F♯ – G♭ takes place from fig. 2 to fig. 4; it remains continually prominent throughout the first two variations, and at the opening of the third variation (fig. 14) appears to be established as a new 'tonic' within the same primary relationship. This is heard now as a modal 'leading-note' one, now as part of a pattern of open fifths; in the latter case the equidistant C♯ becomes as important as it is otherwise in a variety of quasi-tonal rôles — among which is its 'subdominant' sense at fig. 19 before the cadence onto a 'tonic'-based final chord highly enriched with superimposed echoes of previous relationships. Im-

Ex. 3

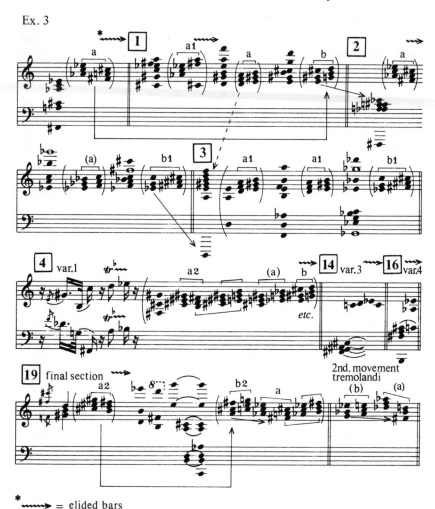

*⤳ = elided bars

mediately before the final cadence of the second movement, 'a' and 'b'
structures, adjacent though reversed, sound in desolate piano tremolandi,
inconclusively placing the A♭ and F♯ on the outsides of their chord as the
dominants of their respective triads.

The piano trio genre seems to have been a felicitous one for Goehr. It is a
fundamental chamber-music form at least as much as the string quartet, and
with equally clear popular origins. It also contains the concerto implications
beloved by Goehr within a chamber-music framework, enhanced by the
opportunity for sharp contrast within the extreme limitation imposed by the
single predominating problem of instrumental balance. The 'model' set up in
the first movement is of the dominating harmonic shape which can be ren-

dered equally by solo, duet or tutti — a procedure with close classical parallels, of course: except that an essential part of Goehr's solution is the confinement of the piano part to a single line, albeit often doubled, tripled, in chords, or heavily decorated. Each of the stringed instruments has more independent movement in its music: only three times in the entire work is the piano permitted so much as movement in one hand against a held pedal in the other. In addition there is the feeling in the first movement of 'metaphorical' writing: the instruments not only echoing the folk-origins already discussed, but also aping each other — thus enforcing the unity and enclosedness of the rhetoric. The unity is split in the second movement by the strings taking slow flight in a melisma of their own — towards an extraordinarily ethereal and drawn-out texture of double stops, a faint echo, perhaps of the opening of the Adagio of Brahms' Trio, Op. 8; only Goehr's piano, stuck with the previous rhetorical style, is, so to speak, left behind.

The powerful strain of indirectness in Goehr's thinking — a sense of disguise, tendency towards invention of abstract idea before any physical sound — while traceable in the sense of metaphor in the Trio, had yet to acquire the intrusiveness that was to become problematic in the conception of later works. The Trio represents a gathering together, by the unities and directions already mentioned, of gestural characteristics familiar from earlier pieces, so as to give them a force and subtlety not found before, or, in a way, since: for the neo-expressionist language still fundamental to the Trio tended towards a more equivocal feeling in the later pieces following more formally sophisticated neo-classical and neo-romantic paths — disappearing altogether from the relatively bland style of the Third String Quartet. The process appears to have begun even with his next chamber work, the String Quartet No. 2. Even the grotesque vein which remained a hall-mark (percussion writing in *Concerto for Eleven,* some of the dances in *Lyric Pieces*) is given an integrated refinement in the Trio which is in no way emasculating.

The first chamber piece in which a full range of gestural language appeared was the Suite, Op. 11, for flute, clarinet, horn, harp, violin/viola and cello (1961). Indeed it has the fullest range of any of the chamber works, and in that respect comes as something of an explosion after the relatively austere and, perhaps, slightly faceless Fantasias for clarinet and piano, Op. 3 (1954), and Variations for flute and piano, Op. 8, (1959). Comparison with later works show that the fundamentals of a gestural language based on middle-period Schoenberg — especially the Schoenberg of the Five Orchestral Pieces, Op. 16 — tempered by a tight Messiaen-like declamatory quality were already present in the Suite. Not much trace, yet, of eastern folk influences, chorales, Hebrew chants, plainsong, or any of the other antique sources that came to be associated with Goehr later on. Correspondingly the quality of expression is less metaphorical and nearer the surface of the music than in later pieces, and, for that reason, is the more instantly enjoyable. Dramatic moods that

flash by are no less intense or individual; particularly outstanding are the
raptness of the rocking harp solo in the *Intermezzo* and the sharp inter-
ruptions of refrain and cadenza in the *Quodlibet*. Given the essential difference between the collection of 'stock' character pieces in the Suite and
the formal through-working in the *Concerto for Eleven,* the Suite contains
formal patterns that look forward to the *Concerto*. The central extended
scherzo — which here comes across as the last part of an episodic first movement, though it is, in fact, the third — with its tiny reprise after the stuttering
trio, is itself a parallel pre-folkloristic type to the *Trio Folkloristico* of the
Concerto (Ex. 4); and the short, intense pre-finale slow movement. However,
the effect of the latter in the Suite is rendered entirely different by the only
attempt, among the chamber works, at a genuine finale: the device of refrains
in the *Quodlibet* is effectively accumulative while escaping the sense of frustrated drama such a pattern might have engendered later on.

    If there is a single chamber work which displays the tension between the
various compositional aspects described in the opening paragraph at its most
extreme, it must be the *Concerto for Eleven*. Goehr has described how,
out of a general interest in the folk-origins of especially the hybrid kind of
chamber music such as this, he found specific inspiration from a nineteenth-
century photograph of a Russian-Jewish wedding-band. He then chose as a
deliberate formal model the Sonata in A major, Op. 101, by Beethoven,
as an example — among other things — of a large form developing throughout
its four movements. However, it cannot be said that he found a true marriage
between his instrumental sonorities, formal procedures and linguistic techniques; and such increased indirection and self-consciousness in the conception
of the work seems to have had the effect of diluting his feeling for the kind of
quasi-dramatic structure mentioned in connection with the Trio and *Sonata
about Jerusalem* to the effect of a mere constant introduction — though still

Ex. 4

Ex. 4 cont.

*N.B. exaggerated microintervals

unfulfilled, of course. Even though there are continually characterful, even memorable moments, each movement reinforces the effect on a different level: the finale, as mentioned previously, merely echoes the first movement's rôle as introduction to the scherzo, which itself gets under way so hesitantly that by the time it has done so we have the *Trio Folkloristico* and the scherzo's truncated reprise. The short slow movement is an echo of that type characterised by intense harmonic working and labelled by Beethoven as *Introduzione* in the *Waldstein* Sonata as well as in Op. 101.

Occupying a position perhaps more nearly equivalent to the Trio, among the chamber works, is the String Quartet No. 2. Its formal ingredients are similar to those of the slightly earlier work, but have more smoothness and symmetry. The scherzo not only provides a light centrepiece between the relative intensities of the first and last movements, but is itself necessary to balance the mini-allegro-finale at the end of the first-movement variations; the latter in turn affects the nature of the last movement's anticipatory conclusion already mentioned. The work shows, therefore, the beginnings of development towards the formalization of the *Concerto for Eleven* and beyond, with some corresponding defusing of dramatic rhetoric. The intensity of the material nevertheless remains as yet unaffected, particularly in the opening slow variations. This movement develops the still embryonic idea in the first movement of the Trio, of working towards a nadir rather than a climax — a formal shape made much of later in *Metamorphosis/Dance*. Given such a dilution of dramatic language, what is left in the still, dark centre of the movement is a concentration of the extraordinarily tender intimacy which is the pervading tone of the work. The feeling conveyed is perhaps of the same order as the reflections of intimate events in the quartets of Janáček — an admitted influence on Goehr — and Berg's *Lyric Suite,* with which there are some stylistic resemblances, particularly in the last two movements, in Goehr's quartet.

The Orchestral Music

JULIAN RUSHTON

If the rest of Alexander Goehr's output were lost, the orchestral music could still fairly demonstrate the direction of his thought. Among his pre-occupations has certainly been the regeneration of traditional aspects of music: melodic continuity, harmony, the symphony orchestra, forms such as variations, chaconne, and even the sonata. His taste for both variation and repetition has led him to evolve intricate techniques of metamorphosis, not merely of themes but of whole sections of music, a symphonic technique adumbrated in the 19th century (for example in Schubert's *Wanderer Fantasia)* and which may be most readily observed in the Three Pieces (Op. 21a) from *Arden muss sterben.* The third of these is a distorted version of the first, and may thus be experienced both as a new movement and a reprise. However, if Goehr might be called conservative, the word must not preclude recognition of the positive nature of his development, in which each step has been towards an idiom at once broader and more idiosyncratic; a consistent *advance* from what, in the mid-1950s, must have been regarded as an 'advanced' (if not 'avant-garde') position.

Only hindsight could perceive any sign of this in his first orchestral work, the Fantasia, Op. 4, which occupied him during the four years 1954-8. It is a creditable attempt to sustain interest over ten minutes or so of almost seamless, athematic music. Its harmonic consistency is of the negative kind typical of the period: avoidance of octaves, excess of major sevenths. Today, therefore, it hardly sounds like Goehr. Already in *Hecuba's Lament* the octave has returned, at least for rhetorical emphasis (fig. 24); in the Violin Concerto it is normal, and in this work personal methods of generating harmonies make themselves felt. The scoring of the Fantasia is also dated, if not quite 1950s-ish pointillistic; but the careful application of colour, the variation of a single note by non-motivic repetition and change of instrumentation, is something which, for all its origins in Schoenberg's Five Orchestral Pieces, Op. 16, will later be turned by Goehr to very personal ends.

Both the Fantasia and *Hecuba's Lament,* Op. 12, require a perhaps wastefully large orchestra, almost identical in constitution. At its best the scoring follows the Schoenbergian ideal of an outsize chamber group, and 'auxiliary' instruments − piccolo, cor anglais, bass and E♭ clarinets, double bassoon − are given unusual prominence not for effect but for their particular range and expressive qualities. String solos are extensively used, and the *Lament* includes brief interventions from a saxophone and cornet. The fortissimo is less well characterised than the quieter music; it is again only in the Violin Concerto, Op. 13, where the orchestra is Brahmsian plus sparingly employed percussion, that the tutti becomes a wholly characteristic ensemble of individuals, penetrated, as it were, by the chamber-music ideal. In the Concerto, as ever in Goehr, the horn writing is admirably resourceful, but its greatest triumph is possibly the rediscovery of the homogeneous body of strings, used as the norm from which the second movement so dramatically departs. In his next works, Goehr seemed to strip the orchestra down, concentrating his invention into reduced ensembles before reassembling the traditional proportions. Besides strings, the *Little Symphony,* Op. 15, uses a strange ensemble of piccolo (also flute), two oboes, clarinet, bass clarinet, two horns and tuba (no percussion). The abrasive and prickly third movement (scherzo), with its fine thin sound of piccolo and oboes, the extraordinary plucked effect of the high bass clarinet octaves (from bar 12), the austere yet mellifluous horns of the trio (148), are still as refreshing as ever; the restricted ensemble seems to be less a limitation than a stimulus to the composer's imagination.

In *Pastorals,* Op. 19, the woodwind is reduced to alto flute and clarinet in C, for which the composer rightly insists the suaver B♭ instrument must not be substituted. The work is primarily for brass, strings, and percussion. Towards the end the brass is divided into three 'Gabrieli' choirs, of four horns and tuba, and (twice) two trumpets and two trombones. The strings are 24 violins and 12 cellos, and are divided in ways too varied to detail. Every cellist is a soloist. The percussion is nearly all unpitched, and the meticulousness of its use recalls Varèse; one of the most remarkable sonorities in Goehr is the passage for 12 cellos and four high-hats (248-266). This is Goehr's most radical departure from the traditional orchestra. The *Romanza,* Op. 24, and Piano Concerto, Op. 33, use an ensemble hand-picked for the composer's purpose, with more 'auxiliary' than normal woodwind. The former has one section of violins, variously subdivided. The *Konzertstück,* Op. 26, in complete contrast, uses a Haydn orchestra without even trumpets and drums. With piccolo used more than the flute, and two each of oboes, horns, and bassoons, the composer delights in the brittle and brilliant results of handling them in his own way, rather than as an exercise in neo-classicism. With the *Symphony in One Movement,* Op. 29, and *Metamorphosis/Dance,* Op. 36, the orchestra of *Hecuba's Lament* is back, with more percussion, but purged by the intervening works of any tendency to fall back on received practice, so that one can speak of Goehr's, as one says Wagner's, orchestra. The process was less radical than that which, by way of *King Priam,* separates Tippett's Third Symphony from his Second, but it occurred earlier in Goehr's career, and it is the more remarkable in that the orchestral technique rejected was one thoroughly up-to-date and — dare one say — relatively easy to apply.

Like his scoring, Goehr's forms began by conforming to the habits of the period. The Fantasia is a web of short motivic fragments, scarcely ever repeated, in conformity with its instrumental and harmonic style. Some kind of modification, even simplification, is already apparent in *Hecuba's Lament*, which abounds with hints of the later Goehr. His interest in alternating tempi appears in the second section, where the ideas, a harsh allegro and an expressionistic susurration, are perhaps too sharply distinguished to make a satisfying entity. More significant is the organization of the first movement. The opening flicker of clarinet and harp is used as punctuation, and in the main melodic line a single sonority frequently recurs – the bass clarinet, sometimes doubled eloquently by cor anglais – as at the very end of the work. The opening suggests a Stravinskian stratification of serial material. The melody unfolds over a pedal d♭, but at the 12th note music for horns and double-bass takes over, also 12 notes long; at fig. 2 the monody resumes, at once a repeat and an extension. Only then are series superimposed, significantly like a *cantus firmus* and its counterpoint. Throughout *Hecuba's Lament* the rhythms are clearer-cut, the gestures larger than in the Fantasia. It was based on ideas for an opera on *The Trojan Women* of Euripides, and the exigencies of the drama may well have dictated this more direct, and more emotional, idiom. The richer palette of expressive intervals and the melodic continuity no longer belong to the pin-point orchestral style of the fifties.

The method of reference back to a point of departure, in the *Lament*, foreshadows later, more precise formal articulations. The first movement of the Violin Concerto is a sort of variation movement on the 'cantus', thus named in the score, which, unaccompanied, opens and closes the movement. At its first repetition (9) the line begins to be doubled and decorated, as it moves from horn, to trumpet, to octave strings, and back. The solo wind counterpoint against the strings recurs at 44, an explicit reprise transposed a tritone and differently extended; while 78 refers back to 27. These links serve to underline the cumulative growth of the movement and to guide the ear through its disconcerting alternation of complex textures with silence. The resolution of these opposites, temporarily quelled by the final solo statement of the cantus with its calming intervention from the horns, is left to the far longer second movement.

From the almost covert variations of the Concerto to the explicitly numbered chorale-variations of the *Little Symphony* was a courageous, rather than a long, step. Composed in memory of Walter Goehr, the work was first given at the York Festival; performance in the resonant cavern of the Minster required further clarifications of which the C major ending to the scherzo is only a superficial symptom, and which seem to have fulfilled a creative need far deeper than the exigencies of the occasion. The work marks an outstanding advance on every front, most especially harmony. The first movement is a 19-bar chorale, carefully laid out for strings alone—Ex. 1 (a). It stands on its own because it is the 'exposition' for the whole work; not only the 'theme' of the variations (second movement) but the main material of the fourth, and decidedly audible in the third (the trio section). Its four-note chords form progressions which can readily be heard behind their manifold developments and transformations. The variations are as much on the harmony as the melody; indeed in the last variation (XVIII) Ex. 1 (b), and that

Ex. 1(a)

Ex. 1(b)

Ex. 1(b) cont.

of the *Little Music for Strings* (Op. 16, first movement, VI), the melody is reduced to a single note round which the chords appear in changed relationship to each other. At the same time the last variation recapitulates the rhythm of the first in the Symphony, and of the theme in the *Little Music*. In Op. 16 the theme and each of the five variations are exactly repeated, another snub to dogmatic modernism, and aid to clarity of communication.

Goehr's interest in variation-form bore further fruit in his Op. 18, 20 and 23, as well as works to be discussed later. He has been at least as concerned with a less homogeneous type of form which recalls not the classical but the 19th-century dualistic sonata idea, the reconciliation of opposites. From his commitment to serialism, far from dogmatic and by now completely idiosyncratic, follows an interest in making much out of a little. As he says, in seeking the right form for an initial idea, "Each attempt – a group of notes, a series of chords, a rhythm, even a grouping of instruments – is followed by a kind of opposite".[1] This he has often employed with an abundance of contrasting materials and even speeds. His major symphonic achievement

1. 'Ascents and Descents', *The Listener*, 14 May 1970, p.662.

before Op. 15 is the second movement of the Violin Concerto. Bayan Northcott has suggested that a modification of sonata form lies behind it[2], but this is counterpointed by the technique of returns to, or nearly to, points of departure, a strophic tendency reflected in variation forms as well. The dramatic pattern seems to be a conflict of normality with violent intrusions. The fixed point is the contrapuntal opening on strings in what could be Alla breve metre (2/2), as similar material in the *Little Music* (second movement) and Piano Concerto (first movement, from 98). The first reprise is scarcely modified, but the solo participates (46); it concludes a sort of exposition (by 73). The next reprises are inexact, appearing as episodes in the development. From 105 the opening series picks up as from bar 4, coloured by tremolando sul ponticello, a wintry interlude between two colossal upheavals (97, 120). This tremolando recurs, with the pitches of the opening transposed a tritone, at 237. A more exact reprise (Tempo I, 273) strikes out boldly, but is compressed and fragmented; an exact recapitulation of 46 (300) leads to the final stages of the movement, cadenza and fast coda. The alternation of this discursive music with static passages gives us the topography of the development, but other unifying elements include the triplet figure which sometimes precedes the brass outbursts (94, bass; 119, solo) and gives rise to passage work (127ff) and to other triplet figures, before it dominates the final presto. The ostinato elements, on the other hand, repeatedly threaten to batter or freeze the music into immobility. The brass glissandi from 97 are like an impassable crag; the music surmounts it, shivering (105: the trumpet marked 'icy'), only to reach further crags (120, 162). Meanwhile the ostinato is transformed into a chilly wind (135); the soloist quivers in tremolando, trills, leaps, even falling into an ostinato itself (143 - 149) in a metre of four triplet minims, a 'bar' one third longer than the 4/4 ostinato of the orchestra (145). The memory of those crags haunts the music until the glissandi reappear in reply to the triplet figure after the cadenza (154). Then the violin triplet is answered by silence, and the woodwind join it in a frenzied dance at the end of which the glissando is heard again (374), reconciled to the context and so fully resolved in this splendidly vigorous conclusion. This kind of stasis will become a major factor in Goehr's symphonic music. Even in Op. 15, the climax of the scherzo threatens to become immobilized (282) before the massive intervention of the horns. The *Romanza* follows the Violin Concerto in that these ostinati produce a creative shock that is almost as much cultural as musical, since they seem to come from an alien tradition: the grandpupil of Schoenberg is also the pupil of Messiaen.

2. On a record sleeve, ASD 2810.

The finale of the *Little Symphony* is the summation of the work, and includes among its diverse materials a direct quotation from Schoenberg. The slow music is the most evidently derived from the chorale; the opening solo flute, 'quasi recitando', uses the chorale melody and the woodwind begins the chorale at 23. The whole passage is recalled in the centre of the movement, but the heavy horn phrase (17) is heard softly on violins (136), the chorale reverts to strings, and the music melts into the quotation from the *Kammersinfonie* Op. 9. This is no mere musical montage, but so cunningly prepared as to seem almost inevitable. At 136, the violins have the dotted rhythm of the citation; the recitando from 32, which corresponds to the citation, includes the two descending semitones of its melody (d″, c♯″, solo violin; c♮″, 1st violins), similar harmonies (related to diminished 7ths and the 'Tristan chord'), and a similar texture. The remaining slow music is a violin solo, doubled at the reprise by clarinet, an intense, because exquisitely fragile, passage (153). The allegro has a short sonata pattern: exposition (48-83), development (84-118), recapitulation (167), swamped by a return to the chorale (203) which is the basis of the coda. The composer has acknowledged that to combine such diversity into a single movement imposes strains on listener, performer, and composer alike. Among details which co-ordinate it are the repeated chords (14) which provide the motive for the allegro (48); the solo violin sound spilling over into the allegro; the reprise at 118 which sounds like continuation of a fugato on the first four notes of the chorale (112). The second movement of the *Little Music* makes a more playful use of contrasts. Its principal material is imitative, and rhythmically simple; the grazioso (18) introduces triple metre, in repeated notes which recall the allegro of the *Little Symphony*. Halfway through the movement the opening motive surmounts strong harmonies, and is again treated fugally, before dying away in a unison; there follows an additional variation *(Tempo di Tema)* left over, as it were, from the first movement. Finally the contrasts are unified, as in the Violin Concerto, by a presto in which the opening motif adopts the triplet (132) of the other material (cf. 56, 149).

Pastorals fits into no category, and the nature of the forces used is inseparable from the form. The opening proposes a motive without change of pitch by alternating open and stopped horn notes, something of a Goehr fingerprint. The 'tonal' implication of the horns' fifth is contradicted by the trombone, a tritone below; that interval comes to fruition late in the work when four-note chords oppose each other at a tritone's distance (220ff). This is the Pastoral of Greek tragedy, not Arcadia, and the starkness of this opening might recall *Hecuba's Lament;* certainly the sectional structure provides a link between that work and the Symphony, Op. 29. The duet of flute and clarinet is an intricate counterpoint, or doubling, for the instruments work

together in larger time-units and in pitch contour, but are distinguished in
detail—Ex. 2. Every repetition is disguised, lengthened, varied; 13-18 repeat
7-12 but reach a higher pitch, and after the silent bar, 26-42 correspond to
7-18, amplified heterophonically by horn and trumpet. At a deliberate pace,
the ensemble is accumulated in abruptly separated and boldly contrasted
sections (but the horns, traditionally amphibious, contribute to several
different groupings). When the strings play *cantabile* (129), the chords and
melodic curve derive from the woodwind duet, with fourths for fifths. At
144 all categories of instrument are in use for the first time, but without flute
and violins. The former then has a solo; 163 repeats 144, and at 175 the solo
is extended. The inexorable growth of the music through this mosaic-like
structure is scarcely held up by a reprise of the opening (190). The *ad lib.* is

Ex. 2

Ex. 2 cont.

cut off by silence, and the woodwind do nothing in what the composer calls
the final section (from p.48)[3].   The orchestra is again broken down, but into
homogeneous groupings, while exact repeats of music for the 'Gabrieli'
choirs replace the former interlocking sections. Instrumentation and form
here become one. The antiphony allows for distinctness of harmony when
chords are superimposed in combinations of eight pitches. After the section
for cellos and high-hats the orchestra is reassembled and welded by imitation
between disparate groups (267, violins and trombones, 279, trumpets and
cellos, by inversion; 273, the violins use the cellos' material). Catharsis
comes with a torrent of strings over a brass chord, followed by, more silent
than silence, the desolate opening and a whisper from the forgotten woodwind.

A reference to tragedy, or particularly *Oedipus at Colonus*, should probably not be used to trace 'meaning' in *Pastorals*. Even *Hecuba's Lament* is
not 'programme music' in the Straussian sense. But Goehr is prepared to
admit, in company with Beethoven and Brahms, some significance beyond
the notes; in speaking of the original image for the *Symphony in One Movement* he wrote: "This image was not altogether free of literary allusion or
extra-musical connotation. But external references soon fade".[4]   Whether or
not this means that he actually forgets the external references, it is clear that
he regards them as inessential to our understanding; and if he leaves us free to
understand in our own way, it is impertinent to enquire further. Thus the
title *Romanza* presumably refers to the general character of this very substantial piece for cello and small orchestra which, in the composer's words, is
"a kind of instrumental aria which incorporates a scherzo for the orchestra
alone and a lento cadenza section for the soloist accompanied by cellos,
basses, and harp".[5]

An aria one may expect to have a ternary design, but the scherzo is not its
middle section, for the nearest approach to a reprise comes only at a climax
growing from the cadenza (361). This delay seems to be characteristic, and
can hardly be reconciled with sonata form (cf. Violin Concerto, II; *Symphony in One Movement)*, while the through-composition of the *Romanza*
equally precludes thoughts of simple 'Da capo' forms. But the form may be
interpreted in terms of opposites: on-going melodic development (aria) and
disturbing stasis. The latter, this time, is not always violent, and includes
quite gentle music: before the scherzo (121) a sustained chord in harmonics,
animated by rhythmic interjections which enliven towards the faster tempo
(146). The scherzo itself builds to a crisp ostinato (199) and dissolves into
another page of limpid stillness, animated by texture alone (209). In the aria

3. The score numbers as 218 both the last bar of p.47 and the first of p.48.
4. 'Ascents and Descents', loc. cit.
5. Note provided for the B.B.C. before the broadcast of the first performance.

itself a sinister growl of double-basses and bass drum (11-12) returns with more violence in the tutti (41) and becomes a Lion-roar (91-107), while the orchestra engages in obstinate repetition as if the music had been invaded by some monstrous uncatalogued *oiseau*: already the first melodic climax, intricately orchestrated, has threatened lyricism with a sort of mad twittering (51; 361). 'Romanza' suggests the simplest of Mozart's slow movements, the most intimate Schumann: elegance, serenity. To these ingredients Goehr adds a repressed violence which checks any possibility that melodic extension without repetition might degenerate into note-spinning; an uneasy balance which contributes much to the fascination of this curiously turbulent work.

The logical successor of the *Romanza* is the Symphony, for the *Konzertstück* is its antithesis: classical, poised, predominantly light-hued. The static elements are there, but differently related to the whole; the gremlins have gone. The exposition could hardly be clearer, with its 12-note row in the piano at the start, repeated in inversion by the horns at 25; these 25 bars, which include a repeat, are then repeated entire. The static is represented by the inner pedal which extends the last note of the piano's row (f ♮) for another 12 bars. Bars 13-15 are harmonically almost immobile, however animated in effect. The recapitulation of this passage is serially transmuted, still round f ♮ (163). Within this frame is a succinct development of its material (from 26); and after a return to the pedal f ♮ has led to an exciting climax (74), a central section follows, of full-toned melody with elaborate piano figuration. A cadenza-like passage before the recapitulation includes more Messiaenic vociferations in which, however, the soloist plays a full part (134ff); there is no sense, as in the *Romanza* and Violin Concerto, of conflict.

It was in connection with the *Symphony in One Movement,* his major symphonic work to-date in both "scale and attempted scope", that Goehr discussed his compositional interest in opposites, while providing guidance about the form. He does not regard this work as a "putting together of the various movements . . . in the manner of Liszt or Schoenberg". There are contrasting tempi – movements; but Schoenberg's scheme (in Op. 5, 7 and 9) of developing the material of a sonata-exposition after, and in combination with, the scherzo and slow movement, is not used. Goehr, like the later Schoenberg, conceives his work to be a diversification of an original idea, or, as he prefers it, "subject"; hence it is monothematic and its development is more akin to fugue than sonata (but surely late Beethoven fugue rather than Bach!). Much of the work, however, may also be considered in terms of variations.

The complexity, already implied, as well as the "scale and attempted scope", are ample justification, the composer's qualms notwithstanding, for the title Symphony in its most elevated sense. It is a complex work of austere and tragic power, with a unique design. In comparison with the *Little Symphony,* it is harder to grasp because techniques of metamorphosis are more immediately and fully applied. The four opening statements of the subject, which together make an exposition, are not clear-cut repeats or variations; the sharp formal divisions of *Pastorals* are replaced by an almost Schoenbergian seamlessness, with much overlapping of sections. The subject emerges first from an inner pedal b♭ which sounds through the short, restless introduction (the b♭ recurs, crucially, at a high point − 526). The subject is a melody on solo viola, but it is more used as a source of pitch-relationships − hexachordal − than as a 'tune' − Ex. 3. It is its rhythm, rather than its melodic shape, which survives in the variations. These are successively in two, three and four

Ex. 3

parts each of which is divided among several instruments and enriched, as more simply in *Hecuba's Lament* (fig. 6), by touches of percussion and heterophonic elaboration. The rhythm of the viola solo is manifest around the pauses (15, 30, 45), and during the four-part statement (flute, 55; violins, 60; wind, 63). The first four notes of this version, originally heard in bars 17-20 on oboe with the other violas, form a recurrent 'head motive', differently continued according to the context. The delayed recapitulation uses this version, most explicitly at 648, but already at 593, accompanied by the faint pulsation of the preceding march. The end of the Symphony is an expansion of the late stages of the exposition; the same doubling of speed with triplets (66) leads to the huge tutti which threatens to swamp everything. The obvious model for this elemental upheaval is in the Violin Concerto, but with the major difference that in the Symphony, instead of being unexpected and immovable, the even more crushing mass of sound arises organically from the earlier music, and constantly changes in pitch, duration, and the exact disposition, particularly, of the brass. There is no longer, as in the *Romanza,* the slightest sense of disparate traditions requiring reconciliation.

This stupendous passage, after which a final brass reminiscence of the subject's rhythm (687: cf. 16) is dissolved in a luminous dissonance, probably remains longest in mind at first hearing. The music in the centre of the work is nevertheless compelling. After the exposition comes "a kind of development, characterised by recitatives for various instrumental groupings in contrasting tempi".[6] The tempi are not combined, but alternate; the texture is largely monodic, the heterophony pruned away. It falls into longer paragraphings, like variations, beginning with broodings from the brass (unison of bassoons, tuba, harp, strings) and becoming increasingly fragmented as it rises. At 199 the 'head motive' is distinct in the woodwind, and from 192 the recitative ('recitativo misurato') is for a rich middle-register unison of cor anglais, clarinet, horn and trumpet. It returns to the bass, and from the stillness of 218, foreshadowing the chorale at 535, the music fills out and builds towards an illusory triumph, with bells (their only appearance) and whooping horns. This is the first high point; the descent which follows, with every instrument moving from a high to a low register, was Goehr's first, quasi-mythical, impulse for the work. From silence followed by the same chord, the scherzo makes its ascent, until at its mid-point (trio) we are left with the eerie sound of two piccolos alone. The silence is not a cut-off, for the music seems to continue through it, and the scherzo ends by overlapping what follows; yet, and this is reinforced by the use of exact repeats, the impression is given of an independent movement in the traditional ternary form. Indeed, the reprise of the first section is rather less disguised than in the *Little Symphony.* Bars 471-8 are an almost exact reprise of 334-341, but what was low is now high, and vice-versa; the inversion is not harmonic or melodic, but registral.

The reprise works up to a passage of obstinate repetition (528), the second high point, which is cut off for a "chorale in the high strings counterpointed by a kind of distorted march".[7] After the cut-off, however, the trombones continue in the tempo and spirit of the previous climax, while the sustained strings merge into the new tempo, *Grave,* of 535—Ex. 4. The chorale is in simple note-values, while the march is, on paper, elaborately syncopated, forming a regular septuple metre in another tempo, surfacing for nine fortissimo 7/8 bars in the persistent rhythm ♩ ♩ ♫♩ . Not only the metre but the serenity of the chorale is shattered. The tempo is gradually modified towards that of the opening, the inexorable march rhythm being

6. 'Ascents and Descents', loc. cit.
7. 'Ascents and Descents', loc. cit.

Ex. 4 (composer's manuscript)

Ex. 4 cont.

notated in further syncopations as it gradually fades. This metric modulation contributes to the seamlessness of the symphony, so unlike the challenging juxtapositions of *Pastorals*.

Goehr expressed his intention in his Piano Concerto of avoiding the 'Romantic' challenge of soloist versus orchestra. He equally avoids any hint of 'neo-classicism', but the serenity of the first movement should not blind us to the darkness in the work. The orchestra is reduced to a classical scale, but Goehr sacrifices his favourite horns; for brass, three trumpets and tuba, for percussion, timpani only, for woodwind, some 'auxiliaries', fewer than in the *Romanza*. The only resemblance to the Symphony is the seamlessness of the first movement, its effortless integration of the static and discursive. The design is more or less a sonata form with a single exposition, not the Mozartean plan, in fact, although the solo entry, quiet yet immediately in control, recalls Mozart. The opening is a sort of 'call' on the oboe; the flutes propose other motives, then the 'call', twice, leads to a static tutti charac- terised by a dotted anacrusis and a repeated semitone in the bass. The princi- pal secondary material is a contrapuntal 'alla breve', which enters in the violins under the solo piano (98). It develops to a chorale-like wind passage (141) and is repeated by the piano (143) and concluded by the 'call' motive on the bassoon which initiates a development. In this, the material appears in roughly the original order, variously transformed and redisposed: the early flute music is the basis of a passage for oboe and piano (166) with the 'call' embedded in piano figuration; in the static tutti (175) the semitone is on the trumpet; the alla breve is heard, almost tentative, on solo violin (195) and cello, then with more confidence at 247. The 'call', repeated more slowly, is heard on the trumpet, suggesting a recapitulation from bar 15 (274), but development, as in Haydn, continues beyond this point, and the alla breve, all inhibition gone, forms the basis of a presto (356) which momentarily seems about to turn into a full scherzo. The last piano solo restores the original tempo, and the final ritornello comprises three notes of alla breve, the 'call' pizzicato, and the static tutti.

The warmth and intimacy of the movement are epitomised by the first solo entry. The end of the first ritornello is a composed rallentando with an inner pedal (a♯′, 2nd violins, from 64). The piano enters, caressing this note (now b♭′) with appoggiature; becoming animated, it still holds the b♭ until it flowers into multiple trilling − not the last suggestion of late Beethoven − from which the secondary material emerges. The dramatic function of this passage is exhausted once the solo is in, but it is too important to be omitted from the recapitulation. Hence it is transformed, after the largest climax of the movement has been cut off short (310). The piano now caresses an f♯″which becomes the inner pedal for some 30 bars of increasingly lively (yet static) music, leading to the chorale-like wind passage (341); this trans- formation seems to initiate that of the alla breve into a presto.

The first movement is long and predominantly moderate in speed. The second has barely half as many bars, but conflates two movements of opposite character in a manner which irresistibly recalls Beethoven's Sonata, Op. 110. Goehr replaces the fugue with an allegro in variable compound metres; but 'arioso dolente' would describe the adagio as well as Beethoven's. The movement begins with the piano reverting to bar 399 of the first, for a short, rhapsodic introduction. The adagio (bar 10) has a throbbing triplet accompaniment which is overtly Beethovenian and almost daringly simple in its constant use of triads. Starting above the melody (14), it follows its contour, reinforcing its slow ascent and more rapid plunge into the depths. The arioso is repeated a third higher, on oboe (29) then clarinet, the accompaniment a haze of divided strings (4-6 parts), flickering flutes, and pianistic filigree. At 37 the flute figure passes to bassoons, a grotesquery which affects the first allegro. This begins 'lontano' on trumpets, but fails to establish itself and declines into menacing scutters from low strings, bassoon and bass clarinet. The piano is silent, until it takes up the arioso again (88), almost smothering the melody in passionate, declamatory ornament; the melody emerges on the strings and rises to a fierce climax, with flutter-tonguing trumpets and woodwind. The piano then leads in to the molto allegro which rises from its bass register to achieve the buoyancy and glitter it lacked before.

Metamorphosis/Dance, a symphonic scherzo in variation form, shares with *Hecuba's Lament* both an operatic and a mythological origin. It was conceived as the ballet sequence of an opera, and is concerned with the episode in the *Odyssey* in which Circe changes Odysseus' men into swine, then back to human form. The ingenious musical construction nowhere betrays this origin, however, and the first object of metamorphosis is music, the second movement of Beethoven's last sonata, Op. 111, on which *Metamorphosis/ Dance* is explicitly modelled.[8]

(See Table: pp 76-78)

The parallel includes a prominent rhythmic motif expressed thus: ♩♩♪ (♩). Goehr, despite his predilection for exact repeats, varies within variations earlier than Beethoven. In other respects the formal blueprint is virtually identical. Where Beethoven works back to his original melody, Goehr recalls variation 1, at the 3/2 alla breve (♩ = 69, bar 309); the first notes of the theme's 'B' section (♩ ♩ ♩) become in effect ♩. ♪ ♩ , the

---

8. For this practice Beethoven himself provides a precedent; see, for example, the comparison of his A major String Quartet with Mozart's in Joseph Kerman, *The Beethoven Quartets,* pp.55-64; compare also Schubert's use of Beethoven as a model, discussed by Charles Rosen, *The Classical Style,* pp.456-8.

METAMORPHOSIS/DANCE – TABLE

Note: Both themes fall into two sections, A and B. R signifies a repeat. Thus A R B R means both sections are repeated, A A' that the 'repeat' is written out and varied. The sections are not indicated in the Goehr score; bar numbers are given below.

Beethoven, Op. 111, 2nd movement	Goehr, Metamorphosis/Dance Bar number	

THEME

A R B R	2-21	A R B R
9/16	Metre varied	

♪. = 48;   ♫ = 144   ♩ = 69

1 or 2 notes per beat

Values of first notes of the theme:

VAR. I

A R B R	28-48	A R B R
l'istesso tempo	l'istesso tempo	

3 notes per beat

VAR. II

A R B R	62-102	A A' B (*)
6/16 (actually 3/8)		

♪ = ♪. = 48;   ♫ = 96   ♪ = ♪;   ♪. = 92

(VAR. II)

4 notes per beat	Theme 1½ times slower; values of first notes: ♩. ♩. ♫♩ ♪.
Theme starts in bass	Theme in bass
	(*) A repeat of B (making BR) seems to have been intended at one time, as signs remain in the autograph. It is not made in performance.

VAR. III

A R B R	107-162	A A' B B' (**)

12/32 (3/8)

♪ = ♪

♩ = 69

8 notes per beat   ½ the speed of Var. II; ⅓ speed

(doubles Var. II)   of theme although ♩ = ♩ = 69

Values: ♩. ♩. ♩ ♪♩. ♩.

(**) This BB' includes short repeated sections.

VAR. IV

A A' B B'	167-217	A A' B B'

9/16 (as theme)

♪. = ♪

♪. = 92 (A); ♪ = 92 (A': flute solo)

♪ = 46 (B, B')

9 notes per beat   c. ¼ speed of theme

INTERPOLATION
Extension of Var. IV

218; ♪ = ♪ = 92

'Development'

Trills (high registers)	244 Slow tremolandi (Double bassoon, etc: low registers)
Modulation to E♭	♪ = 69, then ♩ = 69 (259)
	♪. = 92 (265)
(Tempo of the theme; returning to it and the tonic)	♪ = ♪; ♩ = 69 (280: tempo of the theme)

VAR. V

A B (no repeats)	286	A B (no repeats)
	♩. = 92	

'Peroration'

Extends Var. V	309
l'istesso tempo	♩. = 69 (double speed of theme)
Using parts of theme: quasi 6/16	Using parts of theme (Reminiscence of Var. I)
climax: $\frac{6}{4}$ chord	Climax (337)

CODA

Partial restatement of theme

dot representing a sort of glissando. Shortly afterwards he uses the distant doubling of a bass theme with the piccolo, a spiky sound recalled from variation 1. There is an overall pattern common to both, the increasing blurring of sectional divisions from about variation 4 (hereabouts Goehr no longer always makes changes of mood and texture coincide with structural divisions). The tempo variation results in a totally different character from Beethoven's — as different as is the *Concerto for Eleven* from its avowed model, the sonata Op. 101. In its tempo the arch form of *Metamorphosis/Dance* is like the *Romanza,* but inverted to fast-slow-fast; in technique it is more like an expanded re-working of the descent-ascent of the *Symphony in One Movement,* since the ascent (acceleration) is nothing like a retrograde of the "descent". It will be noted that where Beethoven preserves a constant pulse of ♪ (♪)= 48 and each unrolling of the melody is the same in clock-time, Goehr changes metre freely within sections, the speed-changes mostly coinciding with formal divisions. These changes are based on a simple metronomic relationship (the common ♪ of ♩ = 69 and ♪.= 92), like Stravinsky's *Symphonies of Wind Instruments* rather than the metric modulations of the *Symphony in One Movement.* The steady multiplication of short note-values in Beethoven is equivalent to the increase in note lengths as Goehr's tune unfolds itself more and more slowly. At the same time chordal doublings are thickened and the melismas around the tune develop in richness and complexity. As the music begins its long return, in the section following variation 4 (bar 218), short notes used for ornamentation acquire an increasingly thematic aspect as they decorate the melodic extension of the cor anglais and bass clarinet. Variation 5 is still slow, but the melismas have merged into heterophonic blocks, used between motifs of the theme like the simple percussion punctuation in the opening stages where the side-drum was as conspicuous as any other instrument. The effect in variation 5 is stifled; the fast tempo struggles to get out and the release of energy when it does — a moment comparable to the second movement of the Piano Concerto — reminds that Odysseus' men emerge from their swinish form 'younger and fresher than before'.

Beethoven's variations are founded, as the tune becomes obscured, on their harmonic grounding. Goehr followed this method in the *Little Symphony;* in *Metamorphosis/Dance* what is clearest in most variations are the rhythms of the theme. The theme is originally presented' as the lowest of three parts (bassoon beneath two oboes),[9] and it is given as a single line in variation 1 (bass and piccolo). Subsequently its intervals are metamorphosed as it grows slower (variations 2 and 3), but in variation 4, the turning point, the flute (bar 178) and cello solos (the B section at bar 188) have the theme exactly, but transposed. The rhythms remain clear despite their extreme

9. See *The Recent Music,* Ex. 2. p. 91

slowness – Ex. 5. This 'still centre' of the work is of ravishing beauty; the development which follows has a touch of the macabre, with very high clarinet parts and oscillations of the lowest instruments (notably double bassoon).

Ex. 5

Ex. 5 cont.

An important ritornello element in the music is omitted from the table, as it lacks a parallel with Beethoven. The by-now familiar static element takes two distinct forms. One is a brief shriek on the clarinet mingled with percussion and stabbing horn notes reminiscent of *Pastorals*. A version of this opens the work; it is given in full between the theme and variation 1, and between variations 1 and 2, with trumpets added; during variation 2 clarinet and trumpet use its motif to punctuate the theme. This idea also provides a sardonic coda, added after the first performance (the definitive form has 379 bars against the first performance of 354). In the middle, the static element is represented by the thrusting figure of a rising third, on horns (later trumpets); first heard between variations 2 and 3, it recurs between 3 and 4, at 259 and again before variation 5 where it draws the 'development' to a close. These elements mean that a too literal adherence to Beethoven's scheme is avoided and a further articulation to the not-quite-circular form is provided.

Finally, it is worth noting that a variation method with a theme most readily identifiable by rhythm is the opposite to that of the 'academic' Chaconne for wind instruments — Goehr's next completed work. There a rigid scaffolding of pitches, however well concealed, holds the work together. In its capricious contemporary, *Metamorphosis/Dance*, while no less secure, the structure gives an impression of Protean fluidity; so as with the Symphony and Piano Concerto, the *Romanza* and *Konzertstück*, works which apparently form pairs prove utterly different in technique and character.

I have said little about influences on Goehr's music. Their recognition is often the idiosyncrasy of a particular listener, and even the occasional direct resemblance to other music is in any case no reflection on originality. My own view is that all Goehr's music displays a thoroughly healthy eclecticism, and it is not the least of his achievements to have absorbed so much from so many disparate sources while finally shedding all vestige of their actual *sound*. Thus while we may hear, as late as the *Romanza*, disturbing overtones of Messiaen or Varèse, we could not attribute one bar to them; in the *Symphony in One Movement* the composer has obligingly pointed to the model for the choral/march episode, but Ives could not have written it; nor is Elliott Carter to be *heard* in Goehr's less complex, dramatically more direct use of metric modulation.

Yet Goehr's works reflect light on each other, retrospectively; to encounter a new one is to wish to experience older ones afresh. This seems to me no bad gauge of a composer's capacity to interest and sustain. There may not by now be much more to be said in C major, but there is much to say with orchestral instruments, with ordered pitches and rhythms, with polyphony, and with our demonstrable biological urge towards intelligible, repeatable forms as a vessel of communication. To anyone whose ears are not closed by dogma, or who is not intoxicated with new resources, works such as Goehr's Symphony, Piano Concerto, and *Metamorphosis/Dance* must be powerful arguments for the continuing vitality of our musical inheritance.

Towards a Critique

ROBIN HOLLOWAY

Now his singing moves towards a climax and brakes into a dance.
(Introductory note to *Nonomiȳa*)

The Piano Trio, Op. 20, can stand for the fully-realized side of Alexander
Goehr's art. Its first movement disperses and re-combines his typical
'punctuation-mark' material through an ever-shifting range of possibilities to
open up a form of cumulative power and perpetual surprise. And in the Lento
his typical parsimony of notes actually produces the effect of abundance;
material apparently limp and tentative is isolated in just these qualities until it
achieves an extraordinary degree of inevitability — rock-hard yet tender and
intimate — something comparable to Debussy's 'chair nue de l'émotion'. The
Nonomiȳa programme-note misprint that fortuitously characterizes the limitations of much of Goehr's music here indicates the essence of something
extraordinarily beautiful. This movement truly 'brakes' into expression, and
its muffled intensity puts it with such forerunners as Debussy's sonatas or
Webern's Symphony. The *Metamorphosis/Dance*, Op. 36, is another, and very
different, fully-realized piece, with a complex structural scheme that really
tells expressively, and in addition a delicate warmth of instrumental colour
unique in his output.

But there is a price to pay for every unambiguous success. The following
thoughts about Goehr's music attempt to schematize what I see to be its
limitations, with the object at least of helping to focus and define, and maybe
at best of providing a starting-point for a less polarized exploration that could
touch on the no-man's-land of truth.

'Goehr's central concern has been with a concept of music not as mystical
stimulation or political exegesis but as a medium of ideas in itself, a human
activity like reading a book: "I write music in order that people can follow
from bar to bar and know that certain notes follow and that others don't" '. I
on the contrary see music as fundamentally anti-linguistic — rather, as a re-
presentation or embodying of inward emotion and outward motion, repro-
ducing the ebb-and-flow of life. Both definitions are metaphorical. The
metaphor of music as rational discourse derives its sustenance from the more
fundamental metaphor of music as feeling and movement; reversing this
balance produces some of the difficulties discussed below.

The view of music as 'a medium of ideas in itself' commits its holder to seeing composition not just as the manipulation of a range of techniques for ordering sounds but as the elaboration of quasi-linguistic structures. This in Goehr has striking benefits. His endeavour to rationalize the post-serial chaos is admirable. His cross-pollination of series with mode has with lucidity and resource indicated an answer to the crucial problem, how to produce harmonic sense from this kind of musical organization while retaining for it a genuine *raison d'être*. So far so good, but now the linguistic metaphor begins to become concrete and limiting rather than remaining pliable and pregnant. For even in Goehr's best pieces one asks constantly, why a 'language'? The passage 'speaks' because the ear is excited or pleased. The combination might have been brought about by a note-row, a magic square, a throw of the dice, or the cat running up the keyboard. But its cause is not its reason; the intelligibility lies in the sound itself, and choices which might have been (metaphorically) linguistic for their creator do not have any direct bearing except in as much as the sureness of his choice compels the ear's recognition that they are right.

Goehr seems to have got this the other way round. For him notes need to *prove* rather than to *be* something, and one frequently feels that music is being made with concepts rather than sounds – that the notes are a mere code for something else. And in the end the compositional results of his lucidity and resource are often oddly cursory. Music written to demonstrate "that certain notes follow and that others don't" has in theory got sound and sense out of alignment.

If the full autonomy of composition is thus curtailed by the metaphor of composition-as-language becoming too literal, it will need support from external sources rather than from within itself. Hence Goehr's interest in parallels to composing from mathematics, anthropology, linguistics, semiology. Intellectual liveliness is especially attractive when most musicians so stolidly pursue their single furrow. But again the richness of these parallels lies in their suggestiveness as metaphor – indeed as frankly poetic stimulation (Goethe, their greatest exploiter, knew this well). The artist who surrenders himself to the prescriptions of 'scientism' puts at risk his surefootedness on the goatpaths of empiricism.

Factitious models of rigour lead to emphasis upon analysis as the musician's chief means of understanding his art. Goehr's predilection is for the method that begins in the assumption of an alleged deep structure in a work, truer than its obviously-apprehensible stylistic surface and its immediate deployment of its affects. Therefore for him preoccupation with style, as with emotional content, trivializes: style is merely decorative, affective content is *'belles lettres'*. But suppose that such obvious surface features were what the composer has intended the listener to take in? In that case they would be the truest content, to grasp which would make analysis superfluous; mere curiosity to see how the wheels go round. Analysis is how we hear anyway; the composer has taken pains to make things clear for us. There are no deep secrets, for everything significant tells sooner or later. If it does not, the work tends towards being linguistic in the secret and damaging sense — it becomes cabalistic.

Fortunately Goehr the composer does not practise what he seems to believe. The surface of his music at every turn offers its listeners the necessary information for assimilating its processes. Nevertheless his idea of music as *essentially* analysable — as if it were written in order to be studied — results again in a reluctance to yield to sound as such. Relish of 'glorious mud' is surely a *sine qua non* of any musician however austere; we do not have to analyse in order to feel the force of the content; we just have to hear the sounds. The near-incomprehensibility of (for instance) the last page of Schoenberg's Variations, Op. 31, is inseparable from the frightful, temporarily pitch-deaf noise it makes. Goehr is incapable of such a denial of aural truth as this; but there is a certain lack of feeling for the physical basis of composition in sound, and there appears to be a strong reservation about these sounds' direct access to our physiological and psychological bases. The clearest indication is in his instrumental colour and his rhythmic invention, but it gets deep into the melodic and harmonic substance of his music and is shown at its broadest in the reluctance to bring the music to a head or to a definite end. Too often his norm of texture is the nervously-articulated punctuation-mark. This would be Stravinskian except that it so signally lacks Stravinsky's relish and power.

However the composer most suitably evoked remains Brahms; and here again there is a polarity between the admirable 'Goehr-the-Progressive', revivifying and clarifying a creatively backward-looking language full of possibilities for a sane future; and on the other hand the aspects of Brahms that called forth Wolf's fury and Nietzsche's contemptuous "He is unable to exult". There is no need to defend Brahms from this! No one would go to him for Wagnerian ecstasy or Brucknerian sublimity; but the *oeuvre* from Op.1 to Op. 121 affords ample indication of his saturation in the 'mud' of music — for instance the utter physicality of the way his particular pianists' hands compel certain musical shapes, his almost lascivious delight in filling the strictest, most cerebral forms with rich textures and glutinousness of emotion (those *Liebeslieder*-waltzes in the Fourth Symphony chaconne!). He clearly exults, in his fashion, in the primary ingredients of sound, and his music (with no hint of the subjective self-portrayal of a Tchaikovsky, a Strauss, a Mahler) realizes a complex and contradictory personality with exceptional fullness. This is not always true in the case of Goehr. The extremest example is his Doctoral Chaconne for the centenary of the University of Leeds. It wears its learning heavily, yet at the same time defies all sense of occasion. What would ring out in Bangor or Cardiff for such an event can be only too easily imagined; but to be embarrassed by the appropriate has a banality of its own (Brahms of course struck exactly the right tone). This single example can stand for something typical. In a sense, all music-making is an occasion; much of Goehr's music seems to resist its being so, yet half-reluctantly, as if wistful and only wanting a little encouragement to be emboldened to join in.

The more natural musician would not think twice about doing the right thing for the Leeds centenary. He would then take care to make it as good, as clever as he knew. Goehr, being self-examining and full of scruples, produces a tortuous half-private work that will neither please nor outrage nor set officialdom a-thinking. A general picture emerges of a composer, very thoughtful and subtle, too selfconscious quite to trust to his truest intelligence which lies in his intuition. In common with many of his generation he appears to have lost the sense of a 'given' compositional practice that can be employed without being enquired into or even fully understood. One can walk upright without having heard of gravity or the articulation of bones and muscles. Goehr has made a musical 'language' but has not so far acquired the confidence to use it in full freedom.

These limitations appear drastic; but in the end they can be seen as helping to define a quality. Goehr's best work achieves its distinction precisely by his putting his limitations to expressive use. Poignant feeling is rendered through starvation of the medium employed, and scrupulous intelligence can make much out of little while many a more abundantly-endowed talent spills out notes indiscriminately and squanders nature's plenty. Almost *malgré lui* Goehr is a true creator, and every apparent disqualification is in the end worked upon to creative purpose. These laboriously sought-out sounds show the benefits rather than the illusions of his kind of analysis and linguistic parallels. Lacking either the music-making machine of the 'figure-bass'-composer or the sheer 'oomph' of the 'improviser'-composer, Goehr has something rarer: the ability to put together small elements into a larger grammatical order, that makes him, at whatever distance, a true heir of Haydn, Beethoven, and Schoenberg.

Goehr's sense of this heritage, and his endeavour to add to it, are the key to his value. For after all he is pursuing a greater goal than any of his contemporaries. Most post-serial composition is arbitrary and egoistic; its base is intellectual caprice frozen into dogma. Goehr has always possessed the commonsense to see through the nonsenses, and the humility that serves music rather than the arrogance that uses it for unmusical ends. Rather than the pursuit of pointless complication (and in spite of a few 'scientisms'), he has an authentic yearning to achieve grammatically-articulated classical usage. If Goehr the generous teacher, the eloquent expounder, the sympathetic colleague, the amusing and lovable man, makes no appearance here, it is because – in my view – his music has pursued a somewhat defensive 'objectivity'. But I recognise that my reaction may also reflect the inevitable rebound of the pupil who has benefited greatly from his master's voice before moving off in his own direction.

The Recent Music

BAYAN NORTHCOTT

After the spate of pieces completed in 1970 — the grand and scandalously neglected *Symphony in One Movement,* the two music theatre pieces, *Shadowplay* and *Sonata about Jerusalem,* and the *Concerto for Eleven* with its folkloristic connotations — nothing new was heard from Goehr until the first performance of his Piano Concerto in May 1972. He himself confessed that its elaborately compound homophonic-contrapuntal first movement had cost him almost a year of effort; others began to wonder about the demands of his new Leeds professorship, the more so as the next apparent silence lasted two and a half years.

Actually, some of 1973 was devoted to the composition of a chamber-orchestra score, amounting to an hour's music, for a huge five-part fictional documentary about the rise of the Nazis in a provincial German town (based upon Hans Fallada's novel *Bauern, Bomben und Bonzen,* adapted and directed by Egon Monk, the producer of the original Hamburg *Arden muss sterben*). Conceived as a chain of closed numbers, not without stylistic reference to Weill, the music derives its harmony for the first time in Goehr's output from a tonal matrix — in fact a fragment of Schumann piano music — instead of another of his serial-derived ones, and might have been heard as an important pre-echo of his most recent concerns if the 1979 BBC 2 showing had not sounded so dim and been so hacked about. But, in any case, the first performances, within a single fortnight in November 1974, of three scores so substantial — and, perhaps even more to the point, so contrasted — as the Chaconne for wind instruments, Op. 34, the *Lyric Pieces* for eight instruments, Op. 35, and *Metamorphosis/Dance,* Op. 36, showed that Goehr was continuing as vigorously and richly as ever along the path he had taken ever since the appearance of the *Little Symphony* in 1963.

Though the latter has by now almost achieved repertory status, its significance in Goehr's output, and beyond, has still not been entirely recognized. When tempted to assess an *oeuvre* — even that of a Boulez — in terms of conscious technical aims, one should, of course, always remember Stravinsky's comparison of composing with snuffling for truffles. Yet in so far as Goehr was about the first British composer 'born', so to speak, into serialism, he seems largely to have developed out of a sense of the incompleteness of dodecaphony both in technical possibilities and in implied aesthetic. Even his earliest works showed radical modifications of Schoenbergian methods. In the orchestral Fantasia (1954), for instance, each pitch of the series was used in turn as a pedal to the rest in a kind of cantus firmus structure. Later pieces, notably the first movement of the Violin Concerto (1961-2), exploited a system of variable doublings, doubtless suggested both by Schoenberg's expressionist scores and Messiaen's modal practice; while the unpublished String Quartet No. 1 (1956-7) had meanwhile adopted Boulez's techniques of intervallic multiplication and the *bloc sonore*. It was Goehr's discovery, in the Two Choruses (1962), that all these devices could be synthesized to generate a serial harmony of audible logic with certain properties analogous to tonality, and his deployment of the new system for the first time on a large scale in the *Little Symphony,* that suddenly revealed the fullness of his musical individuality.

Perhaps because the harmonic integrity of his subsequent scores was almost as frequently mis-analysed as it was genuinely appreciated, Goehr was prompted to discuss some of the rudiments of his practice in his inaugural lecture at Leeds in 1972[1]. Any series, he observed, will have certain internal relationships, such as the semitonal trichord, F♯, F, E, and its recurrence, C, B, A♯, a tritone higher in Ex. 1 (a). If the row is transposed a tritone, so that the first trichord now becomes C, B, A♯ this will, however, be preceded (taking the 12th note in rotation) by a major third, G♯, and followed by a fourth, D♯, whereas the original C, B, A♯ trichord was preceded by a minor third, A, and followed by another, C♯ − Ex. 1 (b). Moreover, the notes B and A♯ recur again in the tritonal inversion, this time preceded by a fourth, F, and followed by another D♯ − Ex. 1 (c). The resulting collection − Ex. 1 (d) − that can be created from these segments, with their common semitonal pivot, Goehr designates an 'idea' since its content has an irregular relationship to the 'symmetrical sound space mapped out by the 12-note series', and limited, special properties all its own[2]. Meanwhile, if the hexachords of the original series are superimposed as in Ex. 1 (e) − a process that may be duplicated through the superimposition of transpositions and inversions of the original structure − it becomes possible to form a matrix of verticals from 2 to 12 pitches each, which has some redundances but many common pitches, thereby offering the limited possibility of alternative harmonizations to the pitches of the serial 'idea' − e.g. Ex. 1 (f). Finally, the 'transformational pedal' device of adjusting each vertical of the matrix to the lowest note of the first vertical offers a further logical means of contour variation and harmonic

1. Reprinted as 'Poetics of my Music' in the *University of Leeds Review* Vol. 16, No. 2 (October 1973).
2. The *cantus* of the first movement of the Violin Concerto already comprised such a serial 'idea' being put together from segmental relationships of a 12-note row not heard in its own right until the outset of the second movement (where it is exploited combinatorially).

Ex. 1

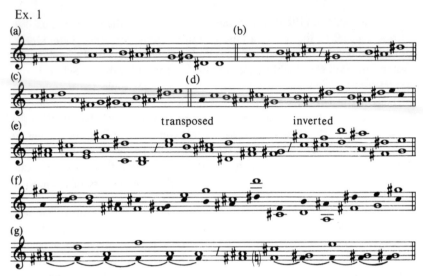

re-ordering – Ex. 1 (g). Goehr has related the latter procedure to Boulez's theoretical proposal for the electronic 'stretching' and 'compressing' of contour in *Eventuellement*. Strictly pursued, the results would be microtonal and beyond well-tempered instruments, but Goehr adds, "I believe approximations would be more interesting, as they would magnify the effect of the irregularities" – a remark deeply characteristic of his whole compositional attitude.

Space precludes a discussion of the vast ramifications of this 'simple' system which, springing from a relating of concepts not, apparently, brought together in quite this way before, must be accounted Goehr's invention in the sense that the dodecaphonic method was Schoenberg's. But it is immediately clear that the possibility of motivic mutation offered by alternative harmonization – a process Goehr has likened to traditional modality – restores the distinction between idea and accompaniment, to some extent blurred by classical serial theory. He has frequently exploited the amenability of such processes to extension on the lines of 'chorale' or 'developing' variations. The fact that the variable density of the harmonic matrix also restores the possibility of the tutti as the harmonic 'frame' of a piece, rather than the mere maximum accumulation of material it has tended to become in much post-tonal music, doubtless helps to account for the continuing prominence of orchestral forms in his work. The 'transformational pedal' device has certainly manifested itself as a strikingly personal stylistic fingerprint, far from the anonymity of much serial music, in those rhetorical outbursts of varied repetitions straining to escape their root pitch which turn up sooner or later in most Goehr pieces, rather like the recurrent chromatic formulations in contrary motion in Bartók.

By now it is clear that far from viewing serialism as a 'replacement' for traditional functions — an attitude that requires the theoretical exclusiveness and cleaving to 'historical inevitability' of a Boulez — Goehr has seen it as a means of their renewal and further development. The degree to which he has been able to re-animate the traditional concept of genres — from the learned model to the popular character piece — as an additional resource in communicating the new, is a measure of his success here. In this respect, the discoveries of the *Little Symphony* could almost be said to have turned him into a Stravinskian order of composer, able — indeed, needing — to express himself by bringing the widest range of procedure, form and style to bear upon a secure, 'given' harmonic centre, as Stravinsky worked with his 'fixed' sense of proportion and gesture.

Certainly few contemporary composers command the variety within a unified style represented by Goehr's three 1974 pieces. The basic material of *Metamorphosis/Dance* — Ex. 2 — clearly relates to the models discussed above; one notes the alternative harmonizations in the oboes of the bassoons' serial 'idea' with its varied recurrences. The principle of extension is, once

Ex. 2

more, variation form – but this time after the proportional procedure of the finale of Beethoven's Op. 111 in which, despite a basically unchanging pulse, the music seems to progress from slow to fast and back owing to the increase and decrease in its rate of decorative, rhythmic and harmonic change. Goehr reverses the process, however, working from fast(ish) to slow – with a consequent lengthening of successive variations – and back, punctuating the variations from time to time with a short refrain, itself varied, and adding a massive 'transformational pedal' coda.

So far so theoretical. But the whole scheme was in turn suggested by one of those unrealized operatic projects that seem to haunt Goehr periodically; in this case, the Circe episode from the *Odyssey* which he worked upon for a time in 1973 – *Metamorphosis/Dance* being an 'imaginary ballet' of the transformation of Odysseus' men into swine and back again, with an amorous, slow-motion pas de deux for the enchantress and the hero himself at its centre, represented by a duet of solo violin and cello. And here the Mediterranean overtones of the subject seem to have lured Goehr beyond one of the aesthetic tenets he has always shared – despite the very different developments of those other members of the so-called ' Manchester School' – with Birtwistle and Maxwell Davies: the restriction of orchestration to functional presentation without indulgence in colour for its own sake. (Incidentally, since the three of them continue to dominate their British generation, an inquiry into what other underlying assumptions they share could well prove illuminating.) Theoretically, perhaps, the glittering arabesques of tuned percussion in the theme's first repeat, the sumptuous harp arabesques and rustling strings in the increasingly magical slower variations, or the glow of the coda's multiple instrumental doublings, could be justified as articulating the argument and its decorations. In practice, they represent Goehr's closest approach yet to a concept of orchestration as something distinct but complementary in its elaboration to the musical substance – as exemplified in Mahler, say, or Ravel. Quite apart from the fact that this contributes to perhaps the most evocative and approachable work in Goehr's output to-date, it can only be seen as a further widening of compositional options in the context of his development as a whole.

The Chaconne for ten woodwind and eight brass which Goehr composed next in the summer of 1974 returns to the functional ideal and with it – at least on certain pages – to a concern with hyper-definition of rhythmic figures that derives ultimately from the influence of Boulez, and has occasionally seemed to work frustratingly against the implicit flow of Goehr's harmonic methods in some of his less successful works. Any stiffness in this case, however, is probably deliberate. Conceived as a kind of doctoral thesis in celebration of the centenary of the University of Leeds, the Chaconne's 'academicism' of procedure goes beyond the decorum of the occasion, amounting to a polemic (rather in the way the attempt at a Mozartian texture and dialectic in the Piano Concerto was conceived, in part, as a polemic against the pervasive contemporary neo-expressionism). Curiously enough, intimations of two of the least academic composers in history, both of whom Goehr has acknowledged as influences on his gestural style, may strike the first-time listener most forcibly: Varèse in some of the high wind sonorities and trumpet iterations and Janáček in some squeaky clarinet ostinati later on. But behind these, more generally, are to be heard echoes of Schoenberg's Op. 31 Variations – compare the solo writing and harmony of Goehr's variation 13 with Schoenberg's variation 2 – and behind this, the looming influence of the Chaconne from Brahms' Fourth Symphony.

The attraction of 'Brahms the Progressive' for a composer concerned to further both the classical heritage and the legacy of the Modern Masters is more than understandable. One suspects, however, that Brahms the first 'modern' – in the sense of being the earliest composer to project his technique out of a systematic study of the past – probably has a special significance for Goehr the composition teacher. Though the Brahmsian point is clinched by a rather poker-faced reference to one of the student tunes in the *Academic Festival Overture* in the extended final variation, the slow, sarabanding trombones from the middle of the Fourth Symphony finale are also evoked in Goehr's 15th variation. Not that his harmony is in any sense epigonic; the basic series – A, A♯, D♯, F♯, C♯, C, B, G♯, F, D, E and G – deployed throughout as ground bass, generates one of the most chromatic and least 'tonal' matrices of any of his recent works. Moreover, although the ground is always stated at its original pitches, its rate and mode of presentation change; sometimes it is embedded in a more elaborate line, sometimes passed between several instruments or concealed within chordal accompaniments, while the intermittent pairing of variations (2-3, 13-14, 22-23 for instance) superimposes another level of continuity. Nonetheless, repeated hearings reveal a characteristic, if forbidding vein of harmony, together with a tendency to build up and ricochet exceptionally dense aggregates between groups – in variation 14, for instance – in a kind of slow-motion hocketting that it would be interesting to hear developed in future pieces[3].

Goehr's immediate reaction, however, was to throw himself spontaneously into the composition of the six *Lyric Pieces* for eight instruments which were completed within the space of 12 days in September 1974. As the title suggests, all six are cast in non-developmental forms with many section-repeats, yet there are also hints of a specific romantic model in the background: Schumann's *Davidsbündler Tänze,* the first movement of which, for instance, presages gesturally Goehr's opening up-beat fanfares and descending arpeggios, and the ninth of which could easily have suggested the dotted

3. Goehr has since made an organ arrangement of the *Chaconne* – removing the reference to the *Academic Festival Overture* in the process.

rhythms of his fifth movement or, for that matter, the running patterns of his third. Yet — a few evocative horn phrases in the second movement apart — the manner in which Goehr realises such models in his own technique could scarcely be more cheerfully objective, less neo-romantic. Projected as a *Spielmusik* of character pieces, the work comprises extended introductory flourishes, a muted nocturne, a porcine moto perpetuo, a curious almost busker-like accompanied trumpet cantilena, a grotesque waltz, and a set of rondo variations with pawky cadenzas for bassoon, flute, oboe and clarinet, the whole doubtless influenced in style by studies for yet another subsequently shelved operatic project, based upon the Ubu plays of Jarry. Yet analysis reveals a pitch organization not only as tightly controlled as ever, but positively teasing in its disclosure.

Ex. 3

The first hexachord of its basic series — Ex. 3 (a) — is explicitly flung at the listener in almost insolently rudimentary dotted rhythms at the end of the first piece, and is complemented by its second hexachord in the 'simple' horn theme of the rondo finale — Ex. 3 (b). But the two hexachords are here interlocked trichordally (the second being transposed up a semitone to the same 'level' as the first) to create another of Goehr's serial 'ideas' with harmonic consequences not only for the finale but, so hindsight discovers, for the whole work. As for the pungencies and tubbinesses of the instrumentation for four woodwind, three brass and double bass, these alone could surely win the *Lyric Pieces* a repertory place as an ideal foil to Varèse's *Octandre,* scored for the identical combination.

After the composition of these three relatively sectionalised works, Goehr turned to the ostensibly more *durchkomponiert* concerns of the String Quartet No. 3 which occupied him throughout 1975 and eventually emerged as one of his most smoothly integrated pieces — only to discover in his setting of *Psalm IV* (1976), a new technical and aesthetic orientation altogether.

*　　　　　*　　　　　*

"I have the greatest regard for Goehr, but I think his music gets worse and worse," one of our senior chroniclers of the avant-garde remarked to me some six years ago: "First it was neo-expressionism, then neo-romanticism, now it is neo-classicism – where will it end?" To be fair, the same speaker has since endorsed with delight Goehr's setting of *Psalm IV*. Moreover, any indictment of backsliding from historical necessity has been complicated, for instance, by the composition of the 'expressionistic' *Symphony in One Movement* (1970) two years *after* the 'romantic' *Romanza* for cello and orchestra (1968), and by Goehr's considerable success in approaching an ideal of piano writing as "a sort of Bach crossed with Debussy – polyphonic impressionism" in *Nonomiÿa* (1969). And, as I have already argued, his reclamation of 'histori-cal' procedures and genres could be seen as the necessary complement to the stability of the serial-modal, *bloc sonore* harmonic method he developed after the Two Choruses (1962) – in other words, as modifications and enrichments of a technique and aesthetic essentially deriving from the Modern Masters. Yet it must be admitted that any residual questions posed by such a synthesis would seem vastly more pressing in the light of his unexpected progress since the appearance of *Psalm IV*.

And indeed in the work immediately preceding it, for though the pitch content of the String Quartet No. 3, Op. 37 (1975-6) derives once more from the harmonic method outlined above, its phrase structure and form represents a far stricter and more explicit fulfilment of traditional models than anything in his earlier output. 'Messiaenic Brahms' one hazards to oneself, perhaps, in attempting to account for what is actually the highly personal sound of the opening bars – Ex. 4. Yet there is something in this after all, for the familiar

Ex. 4

progressions of Goehr's glowing serial-modality are here balanced with a quasi tonic-dominant clarity to support a pair of complementary four-bar phrases almost didactic in their periodic symmetry — if emphatically not in their bittersweet plangency. The result is very much a 'theme' in the classical sense rather than what Goehr has called a 'quotable gesture', as in earlier pieces such as the Piano Concerto (1972) where the effect of thematicism arises from the melodic profiles of certain recurrent, though often subtly mutated, matrix chord-groupings.

Not only is this followed by a 'bridge passage' of solo flourishes for the first violin leading to a 'second subject', reintroduced to set off the 'development' and recapitulated in teasingly disguised manner, but its eight-bar form sets up a regulating principle of section length and textural demarcation that proves to order the rest of the movement to an extraordinary degree. The extended middle movement likewise follows the AABA format of the traditional minuet and though its elaborate and capricious alternations of pirouetting flurries, churning ostinati and chirruping grace-notes are quite un-minuet-like in character, they all seem to accumulate from the simple opening idea of a little moto perpetuo of vamping patterns continually held up by a tiny 'cliché' rubato turn from the viola. The developing rondo form of the Allegro Moderato finale is most explicit of all, even while its three extended episodes calm into filigree passages of harmonics and rustling in Goehr's most lyrical and visionary vein. The echo of Beethoven's 'Heiliger Dankgesang' in the first three viola notes of its slow, chiming introduction — which returns just before the coda — may be unconscious, but in the context it sounds entirely right.

So precise a reworking of a traditional model in a current style is unusual at a time when the general attitude to the past is either to serve it up in quotation marks à la collage or to transform it out of recognition into something else. In the particular case of the String Quartet No. 3, the approach may be justified in that, far from boxing up his invention, Goehr's eight-bar phrases seem to have eased it; but as a matter of fact this represents a change in his thinking that goes back some years. Whatever the youthful autodidact's struggles with Schoenberg's *Models for Beginners in Composition,* Goehr undoubtedly shared much of the belief of his 1950's peers in the value of musical analysis, both as a means of raising awareness and standards in the profession and as a way of extrapolating a kind of 'constructivist' theory for realization as the next 'evolutionary' stage in composition — indeed, his matrix concept could be seen as a triumph of just such an attitude. It was contact, during his two years of teaching in America from 1968-70, with the kind of Princeton-inspired student whose analytical virtuosity seemed simultaneously to deprive him of the confidence to define the simplest compositional ideas of his own, that began to turn Goehr's thoughts back to the alternative value of models in strengthening conviction and skill — to the kind of function that Fux's exercises, for instance, once served. Thoughts towards the definition of just what a modern primer of the Musical Idea and its deployment might comprise were already in train during his visiting lectureship at Southampton University during 1970-71, and doubtless continue in his academic work. But compositional events have moved faster, for with his setting of *Psalm IV*, Op. 38 (a) – originally intended for a memorial service in 1976 – he not only devised for himself just such a model, but simultaneously abandoned his old matrix system.

The work opens with the two-part setting for women's chorus of the Psalm IV plainchant as in Ex. 5 (a), followed by a restatement of the chant for solo viola accompanied by its original countermelody with two additional parts on the organ, followed in turn by a freely canonic verse for solo soprano and contralto. The recurrence of this three-section sequence eight times comprises the work's entire form, with the modifications that from section 16 the sequence becomes duet, four-part harmonization and two-part chorus, and that from the middle of section 14, and in 17, 20 and 23, the viola cantus is in retrograde. But while the cantus always appears at the original pitches, its harmonizations are cast in a shifting cycle of modes upon the 'tonics' F, A and C♯. Thus sections 1 - 2 are in Lydian F, 4 - 5 in Aeolian A, 7 - 8 in Mixolydian C♯ (Ex. 5 (b)), 11 -12 in Ionian A and so on. The compositional problem becomes how to devise a meaningful harmonization of the purely 'white note' cantus in a context of varying false relations. In the free-canon duets, accidentals are applied more in the way of 'colouring'. The progressive chromatic alteration of section 3, for instance, sounds almost like a pre-echo of the work's overall modal cycle, whereas such shifts in section 6 create more a sense of modal modulation between the stable cantus harmonizations. The last canon, 22, is however purged of all accidentals, attaining the same ultimate 'whiteness' as the final organ and viola litany, and chorus.

The 'ritual monotony' of the scheme might seem to echo such structures as the Ricercar II: 'Tomorrow shall be . . .' in Stravinsky's Cantata (and its harmonic method to show a partial parallel with the organ interludes in the outer movements of the *Canticum Sacrum*); but Goehr's piece has none of that sense of strain between the selfconscious stylistic archaisms and the proto-serial pitch procedures of Stravinsky's music in the early 1950's. Rather he appears to have regarded its setting up of contexts for limited harmonic and melodic choice as a step towards a more empirical attitude to musical materials and away from the tendency to see them as individual foreground manifestations of more general and systematic theoretical backgrounds – arguably a recurrent tendency in European composition since the triumph of the theories of Rameau. Yet if the completely resolved and curiously timeless (though, it should be added, continuously interesting) quality of *Psalm IV* suggests the containment of a successfully realized exercise, Goehr soon came to recognise the serene luminosity of its often

Ex. 5
(a)

unexpected and striking progressions as something of a stylistic epiphany too, for "After completing this setting, the material would not leave me alone and I devised a fugue in five parts for string orchestra on the same material".

Here 'neo-baroque' intimations would seem to enter — at least for the commentator who uses 'academic' as a mere term of abuse and regards fugue as an historical form of no contemporary relevance. Of course it was already 'historical' for Haydn and Mozart, which did not prevent them profiting profoundly from their studies of Bach, while the *Grosse Fuge*, the riot in *Die Meistersinger*, Elgar's 'devil of a fugue' in his *Introduction and Allegro* and the opening of Bartók's *Music for Strings, Percussion and Celesta* are only a few of the subsequent pieces to discover new areas of feeling in the 'olden style'. But Goehr's *Fugue on the Notes of Psalm IV,* Op. 38 (b), makes no attempt to reformulate fugal technique itself in the way that Ligeti's quasi-fugal *mikropolyphonie* arguably does, for instance. Indeed the concert in which he introduced both *Psalm IV* and the Fugue to London in 1976 was clearly planned to point historical as well as technical correspondences between his new pieces and Palestrina's *Stabat Mater*, Mozart's Adagio and Fugue K. 546, and Handel's *Dixit Dominus.*

The Fugue's 16-minute span comprises extended developments of three subjects, each of which originated as a counterpoint to the cantus in *Psalm IV* itself – to be precise, in sections 13, 10 and 7 (i.e. the contralto line of Ex. 5 (b)) respectively – a concluding, fourth section bringing all three into closer proximity though not actual superimposition. As an additional intricacy, the original cantus is not only retained in turn as counter-subject to all three melodies, but is never absent from the texture except during their initial statements. The only irregularity is the presentation of the second melody as a double subject with a more restless counterpoint – Ex. 6 – as an additional rhythmic resource in an argument otherwise predominantly derived from long values.

Ex. 6

And yet the result is certainly no simple case of pastiche or of that 'longing to return to the older style' to which Schoenberg admitted he had to yield from time to time; for where a work such as the Variations for Band, Op. 43, revisits Schoenberg's own youthful stylistic haunts, Goehr has never written anything like the Fugue before. Not only does the material yield a cast of

harmony seeming to hover subtly between tonality, modality and total
chromaticism – reminiscent at moments, perhaps, of composers as different
as Reger and Bartók, yet in sum, quite distinctive – but also, more obviously,
a sense of flow beyond any of his earlier matrix works. Much of the argument
is conducted with a hushed sobriety and the coda retreats, in an 'anti-
apotheosis', to that region of tranced intimacy already reconnoitred at the end
of the String Quartet No. 2 (1967); yet the few climaxes suggest a latent
energy and sweep only just suppressed by the decorum proper to what Goehr
apparently still thought of primarily as an exercise. It was the third piece for
the more-or-less hour-long *Psalm IV* sequence he had come to envisage that
definitely attempted to cross the border from 'exercise ' to 'work'.

The first impulse for the *Romanza on the Notes of Psalm IV* for two solo
violins, two solo violas and string orchestra, Op. 38 (c), completed in 1977,
was typically far removed – a hearing of some arrangements of Mozart
for two violins. In contemplating a two-violin concertante work of his own,
Goehr first toyed with the sectionalized structures suggested by Schubert and
Brahms waltz sequences. But when the idea of writing a prelude to his Fugue
by analogy with Mozart's K.546 emerged, it became clear that the best plan
for a concertante would be the sectional structure of his *Psalm IV* setting
itself – which the finished piece follows exactly. The transcription of the
original two-part choruses – sections 1, 4, 7 etc. – is initially the simplest,
re-composition confining itself to interlocking octave doublings, at least as far
as section 13. The four-part sections – 2, 5, 8 etc. – are not only similarly
doubled, however, but enriched by an additional pair of parts for the solo
violas comprising nothing less than a series of progressive exercises in species
counterpoint, working from minims and crotchets in section 2 to demisemi-
quavers in 14 and then back again – a trajectory deliberately out of phase
with the work's modal cycle. Something of the compositional enhancement
can be gathered from a comparison of the first two bars of section 8 in its
Psalm IV form, Ex. 5 (b), with Ex. 7. The canonic duets – 3, 6, 9 etc. – are
meanwhile reworked as a series of freely and elaborately decorated virtuoso
duets for the two solo violins – Ex. 8 shows the beginning of only one of the
simplest examples of this process – additionally amplified and accompanied
at times by the rest of the strings. At 15, however, the increasing urgency of
both the decorative duets and the species counterpoint invades the two-part
sections as well, rising higher and higher in violin figuration through 18 to a
declamatory zenith at the beginning of 19 before descending to the quie-
scence of the last sections – an expressive cycle equally out of phase with the
modal and contrapuntal ones.

The results of these processes are at once protean and problematic: protean in the sheer variety of mood, texture and indeed style drawn out of a
conspicuously homogeneous original, problematic in the centrifugal potential
of this very diversity. The more 'white note' of the four-part-plus-species-

Ex. 7

Ex. 8

(a)

(b)

counterpoint sections have a 'neo-Renaissance' diatonic fullness of a kind that would probably have astonished no one more than Goehr himself had they been prophetically pre-echoed to him even five years ago; the violin duets by contrast present a new and heightened context for the sort of Eastern European folkloristic skirling that has always tended to invade his solo string writing, while the stratospheric flight of decoration through 15 and 18 to the climax at 19 suggests nothing so much as modally refracted Tippett – to mention only some of the more obvious contrasts. It is not the conversion of the work into a kind of interlocking, even collage-like structure of several continuities implicitly in progress at once that accumulates a feeling of frustrated momentum, so much as the strain this puts on the overt continuities such as 15, 18 and 19 where one longs for the decoration to proceed *either* faster or slower than it does. Yet this very sense of tension could represent a fresh means of structural leverage, and I should emphasize that my qualifications are based solely upon the somewhat tentative first performance tape.

In any case the work and its predecessors raise quite enough issues to be getting on with. Superficially, Goehr's current position could easily be seen as analogous to the neo-classicists of between the wars who were once held to embody a temporary reaction to the triumphant march of the Modern Movement. But no composer who has followed an undeniably progressive, if not avant-garde, course for 25 years is likely to turn against his convictions just like that. Rather, the development should prompt us to re-examine just what we mean by such terms as 'reactionary', anyway. Whatever else, Goehr's central concern has unswervingly been with a concept of music not as mystical stimulation or political exegesis but as a medium of ideas in itself, a human activity like reading a book: "I write music in order that people can follow from bar to bar and know that certain notes follow and that others don't," as he remarked in an interview in 1972 à propos the Piano Concerto. Is it necessarily reactionary to re-examine, in a new context, a variety of traditional and historical procedures for defining and handling musical ideas — some of them disregarded for centuries — as compared with an increasingly theory-bound and analogy-encumbered pursuit of a more recent tradition which has perhaps finally run out of steam, and the more rarified and subjective products of which show as little sign.as ever of engaging the musical public? Because aesthetic and even social implications of some significance arguably flow from such a challenge, I believe Goehr's recent music deserves praise as much for its courage as for its many beauties.

Interview II:
Towards Babylon

BN: Considering your earlier outlook, I would have thought that becoming an academic must have been about the last thing you could have imagined. **AG:** It still is about the last thing I could have imagined. I have given lessons to many composers younger than myself and I suppose there must be something in my character that makes this possible. I hope it is not only the urge to make everybody resemble oneself that makes for an active teacher. Certainly, I am less concerned to make my pupils write like myself now that there are more of them and they are more varied. All the same, I often think it is a great irony that people of my generation, thinking as we did, should come to occupy such teaching positions. I am not sure what it all means. As a student at Manchester and after, it would have seemed incredible to me because at that time academic music had nothing to do with what interested me. I doubt if Roberto Gerhard, who spent a good part of his life in Cambridge can have seen much connection between his music and that of the Faculty nor *vice versa*. But had he lived, I would like to think that this would be different now, because university music has changed a lot in itself. In my own case, one of the legacies of my father and of his Schoenbergian world was to use music of the past and present as a direct inspiration. I sometimes feel that colleagues and composers here are almost proud of not being influenced by the literature of music; or if they are, are inclined to deny it, as if it cast a slur on their originality. Perhaps because I was not a good instrumentalist (who could go through the literature early on and get tired of it!), studying music, especially of the classical and romantic composers, and trying to understand how it functions – and I think that if one composes, one has a little insight into such matters – remains very much the other side of the coin of composing. Ideally, studying, say, a Chopin Mazurka, means learning to write it again in one's own terms.

Another thing I learnt from my father is a dislike of the posturing of one kind or another that goes with the notion of the 'artiste'. I hate masks. For me there is no clash – except sometimes in a timetable sense – between composing and teaching. I am doing what interests me in both *métiers..* Composing is a very lonely job so that I am grateful for what I have gained from teaching – the many friendships and the opportunity to get to know a lot of music I might not have done otherwise. University courses, as I have found them, do not generally include the kind of detailed analysis of specific pieces that I like to do. But I have been able to influence the Faculty to allow me to change this — so that I can truly say that I love doing what I do now and it feeds me as a composer. In fact you could say that I am a kind of thief — that I do the analyses for the plunder! I am sure this is true, because there is nothing so inspiring as getting the point of a great work — understanding the composer's problem and his own way of solving it.

BN: Would it be fair to suggest Bach as the closest to your current compositional pre-occupations?

AG: Chopin, Janáček, Schoenberg, Webern, Bach and Beethoven — they all come up again and again! But different composers pre-occupy one at different times of one's life. Recently, Ulrich Siegele of Tübingen University has drawn my attention to a range of concepts through his new discoveries in Bach's music which have excited me very much. The kind of planning he has shown in certain pieces of Bach, and even the concept of the pre-planned piece (which is different from the notion of a piece growing, as it were, from a germinal idea), concerns me now. I am always tempted to try out a new idea in my own terms; this is, after all, the best way to test a theory — to see if one can make it function. This has involved, perhaps temporarily, the abandonment of serial methodology. But I do not like describing my present concerns in purely technical terms. I never liked calling myself a serialist when I worked with 12-tone technique and I would not wish to call myself a tonal composer now. I think this very terminology distorts things. I have not 'seen the light' as far as I know; I think there is a step by step continuity between what one has done and what one does now. But undeniably there is a new development, and that is my concern with what one might describe not just technically but also sociologically as a kind of 'common' material; the way folksongs derived from modes (or modes from folksong!), are common material. This has involved me in refinding methods of composing such materials from the past, such as figured bass techniques — though not, I hasten to add, in any historical or stylistic sense. Ultimately the same rule applies to every artist: he has got to find something new.

BN: But your point would be that a mode can be common to many works whereas a series is special to one?

AG: Yes. A series is in itself an artefact, an ordering of musical material. It is not what children or birds sing (except those taught in the French bird academy!). My own musical development and my feelings about the world around me have influenced me to try to base my music on a simpler, more natural musical material, to eliminate *a priori* transformations such as rows or series. I was already tending to this in the way I 'bent' serial material to serve a fundamental harmonic concept, because, for me, harmony is the most important thing in music. But I think there is a point in not remaining too long with any one way of working, especially if it is such an all-embracing one as serialism. Giving up one's way of doing things, one's props, appearing, as it were, naked and new, can be a good thing in itself. One feels fresh and perhaps the results are fresh. One has to improvise. And the results have been my *Psalm IV* setting, the Fugue and *Romanza* for string orchestra based upon it, and, in my latest work, the choruses, *Babylon the great is fallen*. These are partly fugues and partly refrain forms; certainly they represent a new departure for me. In some ways the results are simpler and in some ways more musically dense than what I have previously done. And, of course, they also represent my first return to that large chorus and orchestra challenge since *Sutter's Gold*. It is an extraordinary irony that Leeds, for which I wrote that ill-fated piece, was the town to which I should return for my first full-time academic post and that I should, for a short while, look after the very choir with which I had had such heartaches earlier in life! The new work is the direct result of the experience of working with the Leeds Festival Chorus and, in fact, learning what I might have done at the time of *Sutter* had I only had the opportunity to find out. 'On revient toujours,' as Schoenberg said.

BN: The texts of the new work also suggest the resumption of the theme of *Sutter* or, perhaps even more, of the Two Choruses.

AG: Andrew Porter once wrote that the text of the second of the Two Choruses — Ulysses' speech on 'Degree' from Shakespeare's *Troilus and Cressida* — was very reactionary, a classical statement of conservative philosophy. I do not interpret it in this way and the Choruses are dedicated to one of the leading communist composers of the time. But the choice of text, as often in my work, *was* political, because, though not a member of any political party, I am a man of the left and my basic position has not changed over the years. My choice of texts reflects a position I feel I want to take — a hope for a better world, something other than our apparently self-destructive situation — but also a recognition that such hopes put into action have generally led to something worse, and the terrible sadness of this. Eisler once said to me when we were talking about politics that, "In the final analysis, all I can say is that I prefer our (East German) problems to your problems." I am not, like Nono, a believer in the direct political functions of art — agitprop texts and the like; I am a pessimist. All my texts speak of a human condition within hostile or destructive environments: *The Deluge, Sutter's Gold,* even *Arden Must Die* I suppose, and now my new dramatic choral work. This is about a revolution made by men who believed that, with power once in their hands, they could create a new Jerusalem on this earth by adherence to the exact words of the Lutheran bible. "We will go up to Jerusalem again, for what was written in the book has come to pass" — that is their dream, and it is the revolutionary aspiration, the dream of anyone who has subscribed to Messianic belief. I think it is in St. Mark that it says that what was hoped for cannot yet be, because if it were to be, it could not be hoped for. This is my subject matter; I believe it is the text I have aimed towards at earlier times. The forming of ideal communities and their destruction (this lies behind

Sutter — I was once a member of such a community myself), the difficulty of realising the hope, these are my themes. I use religious texts here, biblical texts — but not in the conventional sense. These texts are not articles of *my* faith but of the people I am composing about. This distance — the fact that I do not believe in this particular new Jerusalem, nor see these visions of Christ in the sky — is the distance of my own remove from the *engagé.*

BN: But if it is also the distance of the musical remove from the techniques you are using, might these not run the risk of sounding merely neo-baroque?

AG:I think it is too early to say that. It could be — though I hope not. Josh Alldis once suggested that if one is writing a work with a big chorus, it needs a general, rather than specifically cultural subject. It is a 'communal' medium, requiring its own kind of text and its appropriate musical language, and it is no good writing such a work if these things do not coincide. The protagonist of my new work says, "As there is a time of wrath and destruction, so there is a time of affirmation and reconstruction. It is essential to know that time. Now is that time."

Chronological Catalogue
of Compositions

1951   **Songs of Babel Op. 1**
for soprano and piano, on texts by Byron.
Manuscript

1951-52   **Sonata for Piano Op. 2**   **12 mins.**
First performance by Margaret Kitchin, Morley College, London,
1952.
Ed. 10417
Recorded by John Ogdon – HMV ASD645

1954   **Fantasias for clarinet and piano Op. 3**   **12 mins.**
First performance by Harrison Birtwistle and John Ogdon,
Institute of Contemporary Arts, London, January 1956.
Ed. 10509

1954   **Fantasia for orchestra Op. 4**   **13 mins.**
revised   First performance by the Hessischer Rundfunk Orchester con-
1958   ducted by Otto Matzerath, Darmstadt Summer School, 1956.
3.3.4.3–4.3.3.1–percussion (4 players: side drum, tenor drum,
bass drum, cymbal, susp. cymbal, 2 wood blocks, tamb., trgl.,
tam-tam, chinese gong, xyl.)–harp–celesta–strings.

1956-57   **String Quartet No. 1, Op. 5**
First performance by the Morley Quartet at the Dartington
Summer School of Music, 1959.
Manuscript

1957   **Capriccio Op. 6**   **5 mins.**
for piano.
First performance by Else Cross, Westdeutscher Rundfunk,
Cologne, April 1958.
Ed. 10674

1957-58   **The Deluge Op. 7**   **16 mins.**
Cantata for soprano, contralto, flute, horn, trumpet, harp, violin,
viola, cello and double bass, after Leonardo da Vinci.
First performance by Dorothy Dorow, Rosemary Philips and the
Virtuoso Ensemble of London conducted by Walter Goehr,
Institute of Contemporary Arts, London, February 1959.
Full score Ed. 10703

1958   **La Belle Dame Sans Merci**   **27 mins.**
        Ballet in one act for orchestra, after Clement Jannequin and
        Claude le Jeune.
        First performance of the chamber version by the Edinburgh
        Festival Ballet, 1958.
        Choreography by André Howard.
        1.1.1.1–1.1.1.0–timpani–percussion (1 player: military drum,
        bass drum, susp. cymbal, trgl., tam-tam, whip, xyl.)–harp–
        celesta–strings.
        First performance of the orchestral version by the Royal Ballet
        at the Royal Opera House, Covent Garden, 1959.
        3.3.3.3–4.3.3.1–timpani–percussion (1 player: military drum,
        bass drum, cymbal, susp. cymbal, trgl., tam-tam, whip, xyl.)–
        harp–celesta–strings.

1959   **Variations for flute and piano Op. 8**   **10 mins.**
        First performance by Rainer Schulein and Margaret Kitchin,
        Hovingham Festival, June 1959.
        Ed. 10684

1959   **Four Songs from the Japanese Op. 9**   **9 mins.**
        for high voice and orchestra or piano.
        First performance by Rosemary Philips with the London Sym-
        phony Orchestra conducted by Colin Davis, Cheltenham Festival,
        1960.
        Ed. 10725 for voice and piano
        Recorded by Marni Nixon and John McCabe – Pye GSGC 14105

1959-60 **Sutter's Gold Op. 10**   **35 mins.**
        Cantata for solo bass, mixed chorus and orchestra, after Sergei
        Eisenstein.
        Commissioned by the Leeds Triennial Festival.
        First performance by James Pease, the Leeds Festival Chorus and
        the Royal Liverpool Philharmonic Orchestra conducted by John
        Pritchard, Leeds Festival, 1961.
        3.3.4. sopr. sax. 3–4.3.3.2–timpani–percussion (8 players: tam-
        bour basque, military drum, bass drum, cymbal, susp. cymbal,
        tamb., tam-tam, t.bells, wood block, whip, 3 bongos, trgl., glock.,
        vib., xyl.)–harp–strings.
        Vocal score Ed. 10749

1961   **Suite Op. 11**   **20 mins.**
        for flute, clarinet, horn, harp, violin (doubling viola) and cello.
        Commissioned by the Aldeburgh Festival.
        First performance by the Melos Ensemble, Aldeburgh Festival,
        1961.
        Min. score Ed. 10794

1959-61 **Hecuba's Lament Op. 12**   **18 mins.**
        for orchestra.
        Commissioned by the BBC.

First performance by the BBC Symphony Orchestra conducted by John Carewe, Henry Wood Promenade Concerts, August 1961. 3.3.3. alt. sax. in E♭.3—4.3.3.1—timpani—percussion (4 players: tambour basque, military drum, tenor drum, bass drum, cymbal, tamb., tam-tam, 2 gongs, trgl., 3 bongos, wood block, whip, t.bells, vib., xyl.)—harp—celesta—strings.
Min. score Ed. 10793

1962   **A Little Cantata of Proverbs**   **6 mins.**
for mixed chorus a cappella on texts by William Blake.
Novello

1961-62   **Concerto for violin and orchestra Op. 13**   **25 mins.**
Commissioned by Manoug Parikian.
First performance by Manoug Parikian with the London Symphony Orchestra conducted by Antal Dorati, Cheltenham Festival, 1962.
2.2.2.3—4.2.2.0—timpani—percussion (3 players: military drum, bass drum, cymbal, susp. cymbal, tam-tam)—strings.
Min. score Ed. 10813

1962   **Two Choruses Op. 14**   **11 mins.**
for mixed chorus a cappella to words by Milton and Shakespeare.
First performance by the John Alldis Choir, London, November 1962.
Ed. 10888
Recorded by the John Alldis Choir—HMV ASD640

1963   **Virtutes**   **30 mins.**
A cycle of songs and melodramas for chorus, piano duet and percussion with ad lib parts for organ, two clarinets and cello.
Commissioned by the Countess of Munster Musical Trust for the opening of the Trust Centre and new Music School at King Edward's School, Witley, Surrey.
First performance by the children of King Edward's School, May 1963.
Ed. 10858—10868a, 10884(a)

1963   **Little Symphony Op. 15**   **28 mins.**
for small orchestra.
In memory of Walter Goehr.
First performance by the London Symphony Orchestra conducted by Norman Del Mar, York Festival, 1963.
1.2.2.0—2.0.0.1—strings.
Min. score Ed. 10885
Recorded by the London Symphony Orchestra conducted by Norman Del Mar — Philips SAL 3497

1963   **Little Music for Strings Op. 16**   **11 mins.**
Commissioned by the Lucerne Festival.
First performance by the Lucerne Festival Strings directed by

Rudolf Baumgartner, Lucerne Festival, 1963.
Min. score Ed. 10892

1964   **Five Poems and an Epigram of William Blake Op. 17**   **12 mins.**
            for unaccompanied choir and trumpet.
            Commissioned by the City of London Festival.
            First performance by the John Alldis Choir, City of London
            Festival, 1964.
            Ed. 10891

1964   **Three Pieces for piano Op. 18**   **10 mins.**
            First performance by John Ogdon, Royal Festival Hall, April
            1965.
            Ed. 10910
            Recorded by John Ogdon – HMV ASD2551

1965   **Pastorals Op. 19**   **18 mins.**
            for orchestra.
            Commissioned by the Südwestdeutscher Rundfunk.
            First performance by the Südwestfunk Orchester conducted by
            Ernest Bour, Donaueschinger Musiktage, 1965.
            1.0.1.0–4.4.4.1–timpani–percussion (2 players: side drum, bass
            drum, mar., tam-tam, chinese gong, 3 tom-toms, 4 susp. cymbals
            + muffling dev.)–24 vlns., 12 cellos (or 8 cellos and 4 double
            basses).
            Min. score Ed. 10927

1966   **Piano Trio Op. 20**   **20 mins.**
            for violin, cello and piano.
            Commissioned by the Bath Festival.
            First performance by Yehudi and Hephzibah Menuhin and Maurice
            Gendron, Bath Festival, June 1966.
            Ed. 11004
            Recorded by the Orion Trio – Argo ZRG 748

1966   **Arden Muss Sterben (Arden Must Die) Op. 21**
            Opera in two acts.
            Libretto by Erich Fried based on the anonymous 16th century
            play 'Arden of Faversham'.
            Commissioned by the Hamburg State Opera.
            First performance 5th March 1967.
            2 (picc., alto fl.). 2 (cor angl., oboe d'amore). 2 (E♭ cl., bass cl.).
            2 basset horns. 2 (contra bsn.)–3.2.2 (1 tenor, 1 bass).1–
            timpani–percussion (3 players)–harp–elec. piano–strings (8 vlns.,
            4 vlas., 4 cellos, 3 double basses).
            Vocal score (German/English) Ed. 10908
            Libretto (German/English)

1967   **Three pieces from Arden Muss Sterben Op. 21a**   **9 mins.**
            for wind band, harp and percussion.
            First performance by the London Philharmonic Orchestra con-

ducted by Charles Mackerras, BBC Radio 3, January 1969.
First public performance by the London Philharmonic Orchestra
conducted by Bernard Haitink, Royal Festival Hall, January 1969..
3.2. cor angl. 3. bass cl. 2. contra bsn. –4.3.2. bass tromb. 1–
timpani–percussion (3 players: snare drum, basque drum, wooden
drum, military drum, bass drum, trgl., cymbal, susp. cymbal,
tam-tam, chinese gong, metal sheet, whip)–harp.
Min. score Ed. 11003

1967 **Warngedichte Op. 22**   14 mins.
for low voice and piano on poems by Erich Fried.
Ed. 11169, in preparation

1967 **String Quartet No. 2 Op. 23**   25 mins.
Commissioned by Lord Dynevor.
First performance by the Allegri Quartet at Dynevor Castle,
July 1967.
First complete performance by the Allegri Quartet at Bristol
University, October 1967.
Min. score Ed. 11012
Recorded by the Allegri Quartet – Argo ZRG 748

1968 **Romanza for cello and orchestra Op. 24**   24 mins.
*Commissioned by Watney Mann Ltd. for the 1968 Brighton
Festival.*
First performance by Jacqueline du Pré with the New Philharmonia
Orchestra conducted by Daniel Barenboim, Brighton Festival,
1968.
picc. alto fl. in G .2.3.1–2.1.1.0–timpani–percussion (2 players:
snare drum, bass drum, military drum, basque drum, susp. cymbal,
small susp. cymbal, trgl., tam-tam, chinese gong, lion's roar)–
strings.
Min. score Ed. 11109

1968 **Naboth's Vineyard Op. 25**   20 mins.
A Dramatic Madrigal with a text in Latin and English adapted
from 1 Kings 21. German version by Frederick Prausnitz.
*Commissioned by the City Arts Trust for the 1968 City of
London Festival.*
First performance by the Music Theatre Ensemble at the Cripple-
gate Theatre, July 1968.
Contralto, tenor and bass soli; flute/alto flute/piccolo, clarinet/
bass clarinet, trombone, violin, double bass, piano (4 hands).
Full score Ed. 11108

1969 **Konzertstück Op. 26**   12 mins.
for piano and orchestra.
*Commissioned by Watney Mann Ltd. for the 1969 Brighton
Festival.*
First performance by the English Chamber Orchestra with Daniel
Barenboim as soloist and conductor, Sydney, 1969.

1.2.0.2–2.0.0.0–strings.
Playing score Ed. 11093

1969   **Nonomiẏa Op. 27**   **13 mins.**
            for piano.
            *Commissioned by Brocklehurst-Whiston Amalgamated for the
            1969 Macclesfield Arts Festival.*
            First performance by John Ogdon at the Macclesfield Arts
            Festival, May 1969.
            Ed. 11098

1969   **Paraphrase on the dramatic madrigal**   **15 mins.**
            **"Il Combattimento di Tancredi e Clorinda" by Claudio Monteverdi
            Op. 28**
            for solo clarinet in B♭.
            First performance by Alan Hacker at the Edinburgh Festival,
            1969.
            Ed. 11118

1970   **Symphony in One Movement Op. 29**   **29 mins.**
            for orchestra.
            Commissioned by the New Philharmonia Orchestra.
            First performance by the New Philharmonia Orchestra conducted
            by Edward Downes, Royal Festival Hall, May 1970.
            3 (picc.). 3.2(cl. in E♭). bass cl. 3–4.3.3.1–timpani–percussion
            (5 players: bass drum, wooden drum, cymbal, 3 susp. cymbals,
            trgl., tam-tam, chinese gong, xyl., guiro, whip, t.bells, crotales)–
            harp–strings.

1970   **Shadowplay Op. 30**   **20 mins.**
            Music Theatre with a text adapted by Kenneth Cavender from
            the 7th Century Book of Plato's *The Republic.* German version
            by Frederick Prausnitz.
            *Commissioned by Ian Hunter for the 1970 City of London Fes-
            tival.*
            First performance by the Music Theatre Ensemble at the City
            Temple Theatre, July 1970.
            Tenor solo; alto flute, alto saxophone, horn, cello, piano.
            Full score Ed. 11164

1970   **Sonata about Jerusalem Op. 31**   **20 mins.**
            Music Theatre with Hebrew text adapted from the autobiography
            of Obadiah The Proselyte and the Chronicle of Samuel ben Yahya
            ben al Maghribi (12th Century) by Recha Freier and the composer.
            English version by the composer. German version by Frederick
            Prausnitz.
            Commissioned by Testimonium, Jerusalem.
            First performed in Tel Aviv, January 1971
            Soprano and bass soli, female chorus (or soprano solo and two
            contralti); boy's voice (speaking rôle); piccolo/flute, clarinet
            in B♭/bass clarinet in B♭, trumpet, bass trombone, piano, violin,
            cello, bass.

1970   **Concerto for Eleven Op. 32**   **17 mins.**
Commissioned by the BBC for the European Broadcasting Union.
First performance by the Radio Television Belge Chamber Orchestra conducted by Alexander Goehr, January 1971.
1.2.0.0—0.2.0.1—percussion (1 player: chinese gong, bass drum, susp. cymbal, tam-tam, tom-tom)—2 violins, viola and double bass.

1972   **Concerto for piano and orchestra Op. 33**   **32 mins.**
Written for the Serge Koussevitzky Foundation in the Library of Congress.
First performance by Daniel Barenboim and the Royal Philharmonic Orchestra conducted by Lawrence Foster, Brighton Festival, May 1972.
2.2.2.2.contra bsn.—0.3.0.1—strings.

1974   **Chaconne for wind Op. 34**   **16 mins.**
Commissioned by the University of Leeds to celebrate its centenary.
First performance by the BBC Symphony Orchestra conducted by Pierre Boulez, University of Leeds, November 1974.
2.2.cor angl.2.2.contra bsn.—2.3.3.0

1974   **Lyric Pieces Op. 35**   **17 mins.**
Commissioned by the London Sinfonietta with financial assistance from the Calouste Gulbenkian Foundation.
First performance by the London Sinfonietta conducted by Gary Bertini, Queen Elizabeth Hall, November 1974.
1.1.1.1—1.1.1.0—double bass.
Min. score Ed. 11279

1973-74 **Metamorphosis/Dance Op. 36**   **19 mins.**
for orchestra.
Commissioned by the London Philharmonic Orchestra with funds provided by the Arts Council of Great Britain.
First performance by the London Philharmonic Orchestra conducted by Bernard Haitink, Royal Festival Hall, November 1974.
3.2 cor angl. 3.3—4.3.3.1—percussion (3 players: side drum, bass drum, military drum, conga drum, 5 bongos, tam-tam, 5 tom-toms, gong, cymbals, susp. cymbal, small susp. cymbal, 3 temple blocks, trgl., claves, slapstick, xyl., glock., wood block, maracas) —harp—strings.
Min. score Ed. 11300

1975-76 **String Quartet No. 3 Op. 37**   **25 mins.**
Commissioned by the BBC.
First performance by the Lindsay Quartet at St. John's, Smith Square, London, June 1976.

1976   **Psalm IV Op. 38a**   **20 mins.**
for soprano, alto, female chorus, viola solo and organ.
First performance by Honor Sheppard and Paul Esswood, Rusen

Gunes (viola solo), Charles Spinks (organ) and the Leeds Festival Chorus conducted by Alexander Goehr, City of London Festival, July 1976.
Playing score Ed. 11402

1976   **Fugue on the notes of the Fourth Psalm Op. 38b**   **16 mins.**
for string orchestra.
Commissioned by the City Arts Trust for the 1976 City of London Festival.
First performance by the English Chamber Orchestra conducted by Alexander Goehr, City of London Festival, July 1976.
Playing score Ed. 11403

1977   **Romanza on the notes of the Fourth Psalm Op. 38c   20 mins.**
for two violins concertante, two violas concertante and strings.
Commissioned by the Scottish Philharmonic Society Ltd. with funds provided by the Scottish Arts Council.
First performance by the Scottish Baroque Ensemble conducted by Alexander Goehr, February 1978.
Playing score Ed. 11419

1978   **Prelude and Fugue Op. 39**   **6 mins.**
for three clarinets.
First performance by Matrix at the Edinburgh International Festival, September 1978.
Playing score Ed. 11438

1979   **Chaconne for organ Op. 34a**   **16 mins.**
a transcription of the Chaconne for wind Op. 34.
First performance by Peter le Huray, University of Edinburgh, 1979.
Ed. 11472

1979   **Babylon the great is fallen Op. 40**   **45 mins.**
for chorus and orchestra.
Commissioned by the BBC for the 50th anniversary of the BBC Symphony Chorus.
First performance by the BBC Symphony Chorus and Orchestra conducted by Michael Gielen, Royal Festival Hall, December 1979.
3(2 and 3 doubl. picc.). 2. cor angl. 3(2 doubl. E♭ cl., 3 doubl. B♭ bass cl.). 2. contra bsn.—4.3.3.0—timpani—percussion (3 players: military drum, bass drum, trgl., cymbal, susp. cymbal, tam-tam, tom-toms, 2 chinese gongs, lion's roar, 6 crotales, vib., xyl., glock.)—2 pianos—strings.

1979   **Das Gesetz der Quadrille (The   20 mins.**
Law of the Quadrille) Op. 41
for baritone and piano on texts by Franz Kafka.
Commissioned by the Norfolk and Norwich Triennial Festival with funds provided by the Eastern Arts Association.
First performance by Thomas Hemsley and Bernard Roberts, October, 1979.

Index of works
by Alexander Goehr